Akinyele's Canada: A Pathway to Canadian Citizenship

Akinyele's Canada: A Pathway to Canadian Citizenship

First Edition

André Akinyele

André Akinyele Studios

Copyright © 2022 by André Akinyele Studios. All rights reserved
Published by André Akinyele Studios, Toronto, Ontario Canada
Published simultaneously in the United States of America

This publication uses the Canadian Oxford spelling of words, rather than
the American Merriam-Webster spelling of words.

No part of this publication may be reproduced, stored in a retrieval system,
or transmitted in any form or by any means, electronic, mechanical,
photocopying, recording, scanning, or otherwise, except as permitted under
Section 107 or 108 of the 1976 United States Copyright Act, without either
the prior written permission of the Publisher. Requests to the Publisher
for permission should be addressed:

André Akinyele
5214f Diamond Heights Blvd. #760
San Francisco, CA 94131
www.andreakinyele.com/contact

Limit of Liability/Disclaimer of Warranty: While the publisher and the author
have used their best efforts in preparing this book, they make no representations
or warranties with respect to the accuracy or completeness of the contents
of this book and specifically disclaim any implied warranties of merchantability
or fitness for a particular purpose. No warranty may be created or extended
by sales representatives or written sales materials. The advice and strategies
contained herein may not be suitable for your situation. You should consult with
a professional where appropriate. Neither the publisher nor the author shall
be liable for any loss of profit or any other commercial damages, including but
not limited to special, incidental, consequential, or other damages.

André Akinyele Studios also publishes its books in a variety of electronic formats.
Some content that appears in print may not be available in electronic books.
For more information about André Akinyele Studios products, visit our web site
at www.andreakinyele.com.

ISBN 978-1-7782870-0-8 (paperback)

10 9 8 7 6 5 4 3 2 1

Contents

VI	Preface
VIII	Acknowledgments

	01
2	Canadian Rights and Responsibilities of Citizenship

	02
6	Canada History

	03
40	Canada Geography

	04
56	Canada Economy

	05
62	Canada Government

	06
78	Canada Laws

	07
82	Canada Symbols

	08
94	Canada Arts and Culture

	09
100	Canada Facts

102	Heads of State of Canada: Monarchs
104	Governors General of Canada (Canadian, 1952–)
106	Prime Ministers of Canada
108	Study Questions and Answers
112	Epilogue
114	Bibliography
116	Index

Preface

"I am a Canadian, a free Canadian, free to speak without fear, free to worship in my own way, free to stand for what I think right, free to oppose what I believe wrong, or free to choose those who shall govern my country. This heritage of freedom I pledge to uphold for myself and all mankind." ~ John Diefenbaker, 13th Prime Minister of Canada

Listening to Canadian musicians Diana Krall and Joni Mitchell, I began writing this book in the André Akinyele Studios, Toronto, Ontario, May 2022, as a companion book to the official citizenship study guide *Discover Canada: The Rights and Responsibilities of Citizenship*. I figured, if I had to study for the test, I knew documenting the knowledge learned in a cohesive, detailed book, while referencing the official study guide, would help newcomers also seeking Canadian citizenship. The idea is to assist those adults 18 and over wanting to become Canadian Citizens and those who have to take the citizenship test. After moving from the United States of America to Canada in January 2017, becoming a permanent resident in October 2019, and applying for Canadian citizenship in May 2022, I began studying for the citizenship test and needed a way to absorb the information. As a person with obsessive-compulsive disorder (OCD), this book was born and I offer it to you—future Canadian citizens.

Pathway To Canadian Citizenship

In order to become a Canadian citizen one must apply for citizenship, prepare and take the citizenship test (if applicable) and interview, and take the Oath of citizenship in a ceremony. As of this publication, most applicants must be a permanent resident, have lived in Canada for at least three (3) out of the last five (5) years (1,095 days), have filed their taxes, pass a citizenship test, and prove their language skills in English or French. Whether you have to take the test depends on your age and application. Also as of this publication, adults 18 to 54 years of age have to take the test. The test shows Immigration, Refugees and Citizenship Canada (IRCC) what you know about Canada. Thus, twenty (20) questions—multiple-choice and true or false are asked about the rights and responsibilities of Canadians and Canada's history, geography, economy, government, laws, and symbols. The test questions are based on the official citizenship study guide: *Discover Canada: The Rights and Responsibilities of Citizenship*. The test, usually written but may be oral, is in English or French and thirty (30) minutes long. You need fifteen (15) correct answers to pass the test.

After IRCC sends the acknowledgement of receipt (AOR) letter (acknowledging your application is complete and processing has commenced), you may be invited to take the citizenship test within weeks. About 1 to 2 weeks before the test, IRCC will send a notice with the date, time and location (if applicable).

When you come for your test, bring the "Notice to Appear" asking you to take the test; your permanent resident (PR) card (if applicable); two (2) pieces of personal identification (ID) – one (1) piece of ID with your photograph and signature, such as a driver's licence or health card (foreign ID documents must be government-issued, however Canadian ID documents don't need to be government-issued); all your passports and travel documents (current and expired as listed on the application form); a certificate, diploma, degree or transcript that proves your English or French language skills (if you were 18 to 54 years of age when you signed your application); other documents asked for in the "Notice to Appear" letter.

After the test, you will meet with a citizenship official for an interview. During the interview, the citizenship official will: give you the results of your test (if applicable); check your language skills (if you are between 18 and 54 years of age); verify your application and original documents; ask any questions IRCC may have about your application; and ensure you meet all requirements for citizenship. If you pass and meet the other requirements for citizenship, IRCC may: give you a ceremony date at the same time they give you the test results or email or send you a letter with the date and time of your ceremony. However, if you don't pass your first written test, but meet the other requirements for citizenship, IRCC will schedule you for a second test. This second test usually takes place 4 to 8 weeks after the first test, but may be longer. If you do not pass your second test, IRCC will send you a notice telling you to attend a hearing with a citizenship official. If you do not pass the test after three (3) attempts, IRCC will refuse your application. But you can re-apply to try again.

My goal is to help those immigrating to Canada, specifically, preparing for the Canadian citizenship test. By providing detailed information regarding the citizenship test, that is, who has to take the test, what to study, and what happens on test day, this can help those learn about the history of Canada, how Canada's government works, symbols of Canada, and its regions. Referencing the study guide used by newcomers to study for the citizenship test, can also assist those who are citizens by birth or by choice to learn about Canada's history, heritage and citizenship. Canadian citizenship among immigrants is a crucial momentum to the growth of Canada, and, because of Section 5 of the Citizenship Act, applying to become a Canadian citizen and preparing for the citizenship test, this momentum is particularly relevant to Canada today.

Notice: The only official study guide for the citizenship test is Discover Canada: The Rights and Responsibilities of Citizenship, from Citizenship and Immigration Canada at no cost. If you have applied for citizenship and are preparing for the citizenship test, your primary resource should be the official study guide. If you use any other material to prepare for the citizenship test, you do so at your own risk. But, you can use this book as a companion to study for your test. Thank you and good luck! [https://www.canada.ca/en/immigration-refugees-citizenship/corporate/publications-manuals/discover-canada.html]

Acknowledgments

I am indebted to my husband and best friend ***Jon O'Bergh***. He supported my decision to move to Toronto, Ontario Canada from the United States (U.S.). After the 2016 election in the U.S., I decided that I wanted to sell our beautiful penthouse condo in Alexandria, Virginia to start a new life either in Japan, the Netherlands, or Canada. We settled on Canada due to its close proximity to family and friends and the U.S. (just in case anything went wrong). I remember, for our 14-year anniversary (September 2016), we took a trip to Toronto to see if it would be a good fit for us. We looked at apartments and surrounding areas and loved it. When we arrived back to the U.S., Jon and I began making plans to move and be in Toronto in the beginning of January 2017. Clearly, we relocated to Canada to start a new life. I appreciate that he retired from his government career in Washington, D.C. to take this journey with me, and for that I am so grateful. Trust and faith in each other and adventure has always worked in our favour—thank you for loving me for twenty-plus (20+) years, and taking leaps of faith and soaring with me, even at times when it looked scary. I want to especially thank Jon, the love of my life, for his patience during the long periods when I am working on projects...all at the same time, haha, hehe!!! No matter what, in the end, we always have each other and the love that holds this union and marriage together.

Special thanks to ***Minhthu Lynagh***. She helped to quickly sell our penthouse condo in the U.S. The same day as the U.S. election results, I called Minhthu and told her that Jon and I wanted to sell our home so that we could move to Toronto, Canada. She got to work immediately. As it was in late fall and the beginning of winter season, she listed our home and sold it within weeks. We thought it would be difficult to sell our home during the winter season, but her contribution as our realtor and friend was essential in making it possible for me and Jon to move as scheduled, thus bringing our final plans to a successful conclusion. Minhthu made it happen, and I am forever grateful. Her knowledge of real estate, personal touch, and friendly approach has been of immeasurable value, as Jon and I were able to take what we learned from her to find the same attributes in realtors in Toronto. Thank you, Minhthu!!!

Karen Law for her unwavering assistance. She helped Jon and I through the process of finding our first home in Canada. Karen is an awesome, amazing, and admirable real estate broker. During my initial research of looking for a place in Toronto, while still in the U.S., I kept coming across Karen's online profile and advertisements, and thought to myself, damn, she's everywhere, so she must be the person I need to contact. Karen's counsel, expertise, and our ultimate friendship proved critical in making right decisions for me and Jon moving across the border. Her service as a liaison was of great value in connecting me and Jon with Raj Hunjan in securing our first home in Canada. Through email, communicating and organizing everyone involved (as Jon and I were still in the U.S. and Karen and Raj in Toronto) was handled with the highest level of professionalism. In 2019, Karen arranged to give my mother, Jon, and me a tour inside of Prince's former Bridle Path Toronto Mansion (as Prince lived in Toronto from 2001–2006). This was an incredible experience as a huge Prince fan—I can officially say that I got to use the restroom inside of Prince's home, haha, hehe!!! Thank you, thank you, thank you!!!

Raj Hunjan for his efforts in securing our first home in Canada. While we were still in the U.S., Raj, with our requirements in mind, visited multiple apartments on our behalf. Through an arrangement with Karen, on me and Jon's initial visit to Toronto, Raj picked us up from our hotel to view multiple apartments (in one day) and for this I would like to express my gratitude for his generosity. Raj not only took us to several apartments throughout the city, but he gave expert opinion and advice about each location. Prior to moving, Raj viewed numerous apartments, photographed them, and sent photos to us in the U.S. via email. He also gave advice on how to move forward and provided next steps. This was especially helpful in selecting our beautiful apartment, that we still live in 5 years later, and me and Jon having established a close friendship with our property-owner. Raj merits special recognition for his persistent and enthusiastic efforts in helping us transition from the U.S. to Canada.

Sujeet Sinha for placing faith in me and Jon as newcomers to Canada, and giving us our first home in Canada. He played an important role in my transition to Canada, as I tell him often, and absolutely mean it, that he is the best property-owner a tenant could ever have in moving to a new country and for that I am grateful. Sujeet has made his home our home, and our experience in Toronto pleasant and enjoyable, especially with our beautiful balcony and views of the city.

Dearest friend, ***Daniel Tondeau*** for coming to visit me in Toronto. Our 25-year friendship has outlasted other friendships (as you know), endured my many moves from the west coast to the east coast, and now internationally. A special thanks is due for continuing to keep in touch.

My beautiful mother, ***Gloria Jones*** for teaching me independence from an early age. With that independence I have traveled and seen the world, accomplished many goals, and have experienced my life's journey still in progress. This I know for sure, when fear creeps in, I remember who the hell I am, what I was taught, and the family and ancestors I come from.

Immigration, Refugees and Citizenship Canada (IRCC) for helping this book become realized and written. Along with my research, IRCC provided further research material for this book. In becoming Canadian, I have learned so much from studying and referencing the official citizenship study guide *Discover Canada: The Rights and Responsibilities of Citizenship*. I have learned so much about this country and its history, and appreciate its heritage and traditions. In partially quoting John Diefenbaker, 13th Prime Minister of Canada, I am forever grateful and humbled to be a "Canadian, a free Canadian, free to speak without fear, free to worship in my own way, free to stand for what I think right, free to oppose what I believe wrong, or free to choose those who shall govern" my new country—CANADA!!! "This heritage of freedom I pledge to uphold for myself" here and now, and forever—as a Canadian.

Grateful acknowledgment is made to all the above whose contributions have greatly enriched my life and journey in Canada.

Akinyele's Canada: A Pathway to Canadian Citizenship

01 Canadian Rights and Responsibilities of Citizenship

1-1. A group of friends taking selfie.
(Photo by Cedric Fauntleroy / Pexels)

Canadian Rights and Responsibilities of Citizenship come from Canada's history. They are secured by Canadian law. Canadian law has several sources, such as Laws passed by Parliament, the Provincial Legislatures, English Common Law, the Civil Code of France, and the Unwritten Constitution, inherited from Great Britain.

Canadian Rights and Responsibilities and Canadian Law

Together, Canadian Rights and Responsibilities and Canadian law secure for Canadians a tradition of ordered liberty that dates back to the signing of Magna Carta in 1215 in England (also known as the Great Charter of Freedoms, including Freedom of conscience and religion; Freedom of thought, belief, opinion and expression, including freedom of speech and of the press; Freedom of peaceful assembly; and Freedom of association).

Canadian Rights and Responsibilities of Citizenship reflect Canada's shared traditions, identity, and values.

Canadian Citizenship Responsibilities

Obeying the Law
One of Canada's founding principles is the rule of law. Individuals and governments are regulated by laws and not by arbitrary actions. No person or group is above the law.

Taking Responsibility for Oneself and One's Family
Getting a job, taking care of one's family and working hard in keeping with one's abilities are important Canadian values. Work contributes to personal dignity and self-respect, and to Canada's prosperity.

1–2. I voted.
(Photo by Parker Johnson / Unsplash)

Serving on a Jury
When called to do so, you are legally required to serve. Serving on a jury is a privilege that makes the justice system work as it depends on impartial juries made up of citizens.

Voting in Elections
The right to vote comes with a responsibility to vote in federal, provincial or territorial and local elections.

Helping Others in the Community
Volunteers freely donate their time to help others without pay. That is, helping people in need, assisting at a school, volunteering at a food bank or other charity, and encouraging newcomers to integrate. Volunteering is an excellent way to gain useful skills and develop friends and contacts.

Protecting and Enjoying Canada's Heritage and Environment
Every citizen has a role to play in avoiding waste and pollution while protecting Canada's natural, cultural and architectural heritage for future generations.

Defending Canada
There is no compulsory military service in Canada.

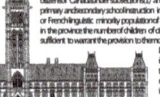

1–3. Canadian charter of rights and freedoms.
(Photo by Government of Canada)

The Canadian Charter of Rights and Freedoms

Attempts to summarize fundamental freedoms while also setting out additional rights. The most important of these include:

> Mobility Rights – Canadians can live and work anywhere they choose in Canada, enter and leave the country freely, and apply for a passport.
>
> Aboriginal Peoples' Rights – The rights guaranteed in the Charter will not adversely affect any treaty or other rights or freedoms of Aboriginal peoples.
>
> Official Language Rights and Minority Language Educational Rights –
> French and English have equal status in Parliament and throughout the government.
>
> Multiculturalism – A fundamental characteristic of the Canadian heritage and identity. Canadians celebrate the gift of one another's presence and work hard to respect pluralism and live in harmony.

The Equality of Women and Men

Men and Women are equal under the law. Canada's openness and generosity do not extend to barbaric cultural practises that tolerate spousal, "honour killings," female genital mutilation, forced marriage or other gender-based violence. Those guilty of these crimes are severely punished under Canada's criminal laws.

Aboriginal and Treaty Rights

Aboriginal and treaty rights are in the Canadian Constitution. Territorial rights were first guaranteed through the Royal Proclamation of 1763 by King George III, and established the basis for negotiating treaties with the newcomers—treaties that were not always fully respected.

In becoming a Canadian, some Canadians immigrate from places where they have experienced warfare or conflict and such experiences do not justify bringing to Canada violent, extreme or hateful prejudices. Newcomers are expected to embrace democratic principles such as the rule of law.

02   Canada History

2–1. Art observing the viking landing in L'Anse aux Meadows, Newfoundland, 600 years before Columbus.
(Photo by Gary Paakkonen. © 2017. License: Attribution-NoDerivs 2.0 Generic (CC BY-ND 2.0).
https://www.flickr.com/photos/paakkonenphotos/42911077620/)

Canadian society today stems largely from the English-speaking and French-speaking Christian civilizations that were brought here from Europe by settlers. English and French define the reality of day-to-day life for most people and are the country's official languages. The French speaking Catholic people, known as habitants or Canadiens, strove to preserve their way of life in the English-speaking, Protestant-ruled British Empire. This helps explain why Anglophones (English speakers) are generally referred to as English Canadians. Generations of pioneers and builders of British origins, as well as other groups, invested and endured hardship in laying the foundations of Canada's country. Canada is often referred to as a "land of immigrants" because, over the past 200 years, millions of newcomers have helped to build and defend Canada's way of life. Required by law, the federal government is to provide services throughout Canada in English and French.

The first Europeans, the Vikings from Iceland, who colonized Greenland over 1,000 years ago, also reached Labrador and the island of Newfoundland. The remains of the Vikings settlement, l'Anse aux Meadows, are a World Heritage site. European exploration began in earnest in 1497 with the expedition of John Cabot, who was the first to draw a map of Canada's East Coast. The skilled and courageous men who travelled by canoe were called voyageurs and coureurs des bois, and formed strong alliances with First Nations.

2–2. John Cabot.
(Photo by The New York Public Library Digital Collection)

English colonies along the Atlantic seaboard, dating from the early 1600s, became richer and more populous than New France (Quebec). Great Britain renamed the colony the "Province of Quebec" following the British and French war.

The old Province of Canada was split into two new provinces: Ontario and Quebec, which, together with New Brunswick and Nova Scotia, formed the new country called the Dominion of Canada. Each province would elect its own legislature and have control of such areas as education and health.

The Canadian Crown (The Crown) in Canada has been a symbol of the state for over 400 years. Canada has been a constitutional monarchy since Confederation in 1867 during Queen Victoria's reign. The Crown is a symbol of government, including Parliament, the legislatures, the courts, police services and the Canadian Forces.

The war of 1918 strengthened both national and imperial pride, particularly in English Canada. Under the command of General Sir Arthur Currie, Canada's greatest soldier, the Canadian Corps advanced alongside the French and British Empire troops in the last hundred days. With Germany and Austria's surrender, the war ended in the Armistice on November 11, 1918.

The British Empire, after the First World War, evolved into a free association of states known as the British Commonwealth of Nations. Canada developed its autonomy with a capacity to make significant contributions internationally, remaining a leading member of the Commonwealth to this day, together with other successor states of the Empire such as India, Australia, New Zealand, and several African and Caribbean countries.

In the Second World War, Canada joined with its democratic allies in the fight to defeat tyranny by force of arms. More than one million Canadians and Newfoundlanders (Newfoundland was a separate British entity) served in the Second World War and of these over 44,000 were killed.

The Royal Canadian Air Force (RCAF) took part in the Battle of Britain and provided a high proportion of Commonwealth aircrew in bombers and fighter planes over Europe. Canada contributed more to the Allied air effort than any other Commonwealth country, with over 130,000 Allied air crew trained in Canada under the British Commonwealth Air Training Plan.

The Royal Canadian Navy (RCN) saw its finest hour in the Battle of the Atlantic, protecting convoys of merchant ships against German submarines. Canada's Merchant Navy helped to feed, clothe and resupply Britain.

At the end of the Second World War, Canada had the third largest navy in the world.

2–3. The first nursing sisters of the Royal Canadian Army Medical Corps (R.C.A.M.C.) to land in France after D-Day.
[More than 3,000 nurses, nicknamed "Bluebirds," served in the Royal Canadian Army Medical Corps, about 2,500 of them overseas]
(Photo by Lieutenant Frank L. Dubervill. Canada. Department of National Defence. Library and Archives Canada, PA-204952.
© 1944, 2006. License: Attribution 2.0 Generic (CC BY 2.0).
https://www.flickr.com/photos/lac-bac/7196115362/)

2–4. Royal Canadian Mounted Police constable checks documents of Japanese-Canadian evacuees, Slocan City, British Columbia.
(Photo by Tak Toyota Library and Archives Canada, C-047387.
© 1942, 2017. License: Attribution 2.0 Generic (CC BY 2.0).
https://www.flickr.com/photos/lac-bac/37102683784)

2–5. Inspection of Canadian Brigade in Hong Kong on the day of arrival, 16 November 1941.
(Photo by Canada. Dept. of National Defence. License: Public Domain)

In the Pacific war, Japan invaded the Aleutian Islands, attacked a lighthouse on Vancouver Island, launched fire balloons over British Columbia (B.C.) and the Prairies, and grossly maltreated Canadian prisoners of war captured at Hong Kong.

Regrettably, public opinion in B.C. and the state of war led to the forcible relocation of Canadians of Japanese origin by the federal government and the sale of their property without compensation. This occurred even though the military and the Royal Canadian Mounted Police (RCMP) told Ottawa that Japanese Canadians posed little danger to Canada. The Canadian Government apologized in 1988 for wartime wrongs and compensated the victims.

2–6. The British Commonwealth of Nations Together.
(Photo by Luntz. Library and Archives Canada, e010697871. © 1941, 2015.
License: Attribution 2.0 Generic (CC BY 2.0). https://www.flickr.com/photos/lac-bac/19694510986/)

2–7. North Atlantic Treaty Organization. Organisation du traité de l'Atlantique nord.
(Photo by Unknown author. License: Public Domain.)

The Cold War began when several liberated countries of eastern Europe became part of a Communist bloc controlled by the Soviet Union under the dictator Josef Stalin.

Canada joined with other democratic countries of the West to form the North Atlantic Treaty Organization (NATO), a military alliance, and with the United States in the North American Aerospace Defense Command (NORAD). Canada joined international organizations such as the United Nations (UN). Canada has taken part in numerous UN peacekeeping missions in places as varied as Egypt, Cyprus and Haiti, as well as in other international security operations such as those in the former Yugoslavia and Afghanistan.

2–8. The emblem of the United Nations.
(Photo by Joowwww. License: Public Domain)

2–9. A Cree man from Lac des Isles, Saskatchewan (1928).
(Photo by Edward S. Curtis. Library and Archives Canada, PA-039702. © 1928, 2017. License: Attribution 2.0 Generic (CC BY 2.0). https://commons.wikimedia.org/wiki/File:A_Cree_man_from_Lac_des_Isles,_Saskatchewan_Un_Cri_du_Lac_des_Isles_%28Saskatchewan%29_%2834407152055%29.jpg)

Important People

Aboriginal Peoples

The ancestors of Aboriginal peoples are believed to have migrated from Asia many thousands of years ago. Aboriginal peoples were well established here long before explorers from Europe first came to North America. When Europeans explored Canada they found all regions occupied by native peoples they called Indians (as the first explorers thought they had reached the East Indies). Diverse, vibrant First Nations cultures were rooted in religious beliefs about their relationship to the Creator, the natural environment and each other. The native people lived off the land, some by hunting and gathering, others by raising crops. The Huron-Wendat of the Great Lake Region, like the Iroquois, were farmers and hunters. The Cree and Dene of the Northwest were hunter-gatherers. The Sioux were nomadic, following the bison (buffalo) herd. The Inuit lived off Arctic wildlife. West Coast natives preserved fish by drying and smoking. Warfare was common among Aboriginal groups as they competed for land, resources and prestige.

The arrival of European traders, missionaries, soldiers and colonists changed the native way of life forever. Large numbers of Aboriginals died of European diseases to which they lacked immunity. Nevertheless, Aboriginals and Europeans formed strong economic, religious and military bonds in the first 200 years of coexistence which laid the foundations of Canada. The French and Aboriginal people collaborated in the vast fur-trade economy, driven by the demand for beaver pelts in Europe.

Aboriginal and treaty rights are in the Canadian Constitution. About 65% of the Aboriginal people are First Nations.

The Acadians

The descendants of French colonists who began settling in what are now the Maritime provinces in 1604 were the Acadians. Between 1755 and 1763, during the war between Britain and France, more than two-thirds of the Acadians were deported from their homeland – known as the "Great Upheaval." Nonetheless, the Acadians survived and maintained their unique identity. Today, Acadian culture is flourishing and is a lively part of French-speaking Canada.

Adrienne Clarkson

The 26th Governor General Adrienne Clarkson, the first of Asian origin, established The Clarkson Cup in 2005.

Agnes Macphail

A farmer and teacher, Agnes Macphail became the first woman Member of Parliament (MP) in 1921.

Bishop Laval, Count Frontenac and Jean Talon

Leaders Bishop Laval, Count Frontenac and Jean Talon built a French Empire in North America that reached from Hudson Bay to the Gulf of Mexico.

Brigadier James Wolfe and the Marquis de Montcalm

Commanders of both British and French armies, James Wolfe and the Marquis de Montcalm were killed leading their troops in battle.

Canadian Rangers

Part of the Canadian Forces Reserves (militia), the Canadian Rangers play a key role dealing with harsh weather conditions in an isolated region. They travel by snowmobile in the winter from Resolute to the Magnetic North Pole, and also travel by all-terrain vehicles in the summer from Resolute to the Magnetic North Pole. They draw on indigenous knowledge and experience. The Canadian Rangers keep the flag flying in Canada's Arctic.

Catriona Le May Doan

Catriona Le May Doan carried the flag after winning a gold medal in speed skating at the 2002 Olympic Winter Games.

Chief Tecumseh

Leading Canadian volunteers, First Nations, and Shawnee, Chief Tecumseh supported British soldiers in Canada's defence in the war of 1812.

2–10. Portrait of Tecumtha (c. 1808). [Shawnee Chief Tecumseh]
(Photo by Benson J. Lossing and Toronto Public Library. © 1915, 2013. License: Public Domain and Attribution-ShareAlike 2.0 Generic (CC BY-SA 2.0). https://www.flickr.com/photos/43021516@N06/8563140546)

2–11. Donald A. Smith driving the Last Spike to complete the Canadian Pacific Railway.
(Photo by Alexander Ross. Library and Archives Canada, C-003693. © 1885, 2016. License: Attribution 2.0 Generic (CC BY 2.0). https://www.flickr.com/photos/lac-bac/29631071364)

Count Frontenac

A leader, along with Jean Talon and Bishop Laval, Count Frontenac built a French Empire in North America that reached from Hudson Bay to the Gulf of Mexico. He refused to surrender Quebec to the English in 1690, saying: "My only reply will be from the mouths of my cannons!"

Donald Smith (Lord Strathcona)

The Scottish-born director of the Canadian Pacific Railway (CPR), Donald Smith (Lord Strathcona) drove the last spike on November 7, 1885, a powerful symbol of unity completed.

Dr. Emily Stowe

The founder of the Women's Suffrage Movement in Canada, Dr. Emily Stowe was the first Canadian woman to practise medicine in Canada.

The Duke of Wellington

The Duke of Wellington sent some of his best soldiers to defend Canada in 1814. He helped create Bytown — as the endpoint of the Rideau Canal, Bytown (former name of Ottawa) was part of a network of forts to prevent the United States of America (U.S.A.) from invading Canada again. Wellington, in his defeat of Napoleon in 1815, played a direct role in founding the national capital – Ottawa.

Emily Carr

Emily Carr painted the forests and Aboriginal artifacts of the West Coast.

The Fathers of Confederation

Establishing the Dominion of Canada on July 1, 1867, the birth of the country that we know today, The Fathers of Confederation created two levels of government: Federal and Provincial.

Founding Peoples

Canada's three (3) founding peoples are the Aboriginal, French, and British.

Gabriel Dumont

Gabriel Dumont was the Métis greatest military leader (Métis Resistance).

The Inuit

Meaning "the people" in the Inuktitut language, the Inuit live in small, scattered communities across the Arctic. Their knowledge of the land, sea and wildlife enabled them to adapt to one of the harshest environments on earth. About 4% of the Aboriginal people are Inuit.

Jacques Cartier

The first European to explore the St. Lawrence River was Jacques Cartier. He was also the first to set eyes on present-day Québec City and Montreal. Between 1534 and 1542, he made three voyages across the Atlantic, claiming the land for King Francis I of France. Jacques Cartier heard two captured guides speak the Iroquoian word kanta, meaning "village."

John Buchan

2–12. John Buchan, 1st Baron Tweedsmuir, in ceremonial dress of the Governor General of Canada.
(Photo by Unknown Author and National Archives of Canada. License: Public Domain)

The 1st Baron Tweedsmuir, John Buchan was a popular Governor General of Canada (1935–40). As the 15th Governor General, of Kainai First

2–13. Portrait of Joseph Tayadaneega, called the Brant (Joseph Brant, 1742-1807).
(Photo by John Raphael Smith and Toronto Public Library. © 1779, 2012. License: Public Domain and Attribution-ShareAlike 2.0 Generic (CC BY-SA 2.0). https://www.flickr.com/photos/43021516@N06/7838386000)

Nation, he said immigrant groups "should retain their individuality and each make its contribution to the national character." Each could learn "from the other, and … while they cherish their own special loyalties and traditions, they cherish not less that new loyalty and tradition which springs from their union." (Canadian Club of Halifax, 1937).

John Cabot

An Italian immigrant to England, John Cabot was the first to map Canada's Atlantic shore (Canada's East Coast). He was also the first setting foot on Newfoundland or Cape Breton Island in 1497. John Cabot claimed the New Founde Land (later New Foundland) for England.

Joseph Brant

Joseph Brant led thousands of Loyalist Mohawk Indians into Canada.

Jean-Paul Riopelle

Most notably known as one of the Les Automatistes of Quebec, Jean-Paul Riopelle was a pioneer of modern abstract art in the 1950s.

2–14. Meeting between Laura Secord and Lieutenant FitzGibbon, June 1813.
(Photo by Lorne K. Smith and Library and Archives Canada, e010944077. © 1920, 2011. License: Attribution 2.0 Generic (CC BY 2.0). https://www.flickr.com/photos/lac-bac/7288415868)

2–15. Portrait of John Graves Simcoe.
(Photo by Jean Laurent Mosnier and Toronto Public Library. © 1791, 2012. License: Public Domain and Attribution-ShareAlike 2.0 Generic (CC BY-SA 2.0). https://www.flickr.com/photos43021516@N06/7838470522)

2–16. Lieutenant-Colonel Charles de Salaberry.
(Photo by Anson Dickinson, Asher Brown Durand, and Library and Archives Canada, e010958146. © 1824–25, 2012. License: Attribution 2.0 Generic (CC BY 2.0). https://www.flickr.com/photos/lac-bac/6836780213)

King George V

King George V assigned Canada's national colours (white and red) in 1921, colours of the national flag today. In 1923, his portrait appeared on the Dominion of Canada $1 bills.

Laura Secord

In 1813, Laura Secord made a dangerous 19-mile (30-km) journey on foot to warn Lieutenant James FitzGibbon of a planned American attack. Her bravery contributed to victory at the Battle of Beaver Dams. Laura Secord is recognized as a heroine to this day.

Lieutenant-Colonel Charles de Salaberry

In 1813, Lieutenant-Colonel Charles de Salaberry and around 460 soldiers, mostly French Canadiens, turned back about 4,000 American invaders at Chateauguay, south of Montreal.

Lieutenant-Colonel John Graves Simcoe

Upper Canada's (later Ontario's) first Lieutenant Governor was Lieutenant-Colonel John Graves Simcoe. He was founder of the City of York (now Toronto). Led by Simcoe, a Loyalist military officer, in 1793, Upper Canada became the first province in the Empire to move toward abolition of slavery. Thus, Simcoe made Upper Canada the first province in the British Empire to abolish slavery.

2–17. United Empire Loyalist plaque in stone in Hamilton, Ontario in memory of Col. Richard Beasley.
(Photo by Laslovarga. © 2011. License: Attribution-ShareAlike 3.0 Unported (CC BY-SA 3.0). https://commons.wikimedia.org/wiki/File:United_Empire_Loyalist_plaque_in_stone_in_Hamilton,_Ontario.jpg)

Lord Durham

An English reformer, Lord Durham was sent to report on the rebellions. He recommended that Upper Canada (later Ontario) and Lower Canada (later Quebec) be merged and given responsible government, which meant that the ministers of the Crown must have the support of a majority of the elected representatives in order to govern.

Lord Durham controversially said that the quickest way for the Canadiens to achieve progress was to assimilate into English-speaking Protestant culture. This recommendation demonstrated a complete lack of understanding of French Canadians, who sought to uphold the distinct identity of French Canada.

Lord Grey

The Governor General Lord Grey, in 1909, donated the championship Grey Cup for Professional teams competing in the Canadian Football League (CFL).

Lord Stanley

The Governor General Lord Stanley, in 1892, donated the Stanley Cup to the National Hockey League that played for the championship Stanley Cup.

Louis Riel

Leading an armed uprising, Louis Riel seized Fort Garry (the territorial capital). He fled to the United States. And, Canada established a new province: Manitoba. Riel is seen by many as a hero, a defender of Métis rights, and the father of Manitoba. He was elected to Parliament but never took his seat. Later, as Métis and Indian rights were again threatened by westward settlement, a second rebellion in 1885, in present-day Saskatchewan, led to his trial and execution for high treason, a decision that was strongly opposed in Quebec.

Loyalists

More than 40,000 people loyal to the Crown, called "Loyalists," fled the oppression of the American Revolution to settle in Nova Scotia and Quebec – North America was again divided by war. About 3,000 black Loyalists, freedmen and slaves came north seeking a better life. Moreover, the Loyalists came from Dutch, German, British, Scandinavian, Aboriginal and other origins and from Presbyterian, Anglican, Baptist, Methodist, Jewish, Quaker and Catholic religious backgrounds.

2–18. Col. S.B. Steele commanding Strathcona's Horse. No. 733 (1900). [Major-General Sir Sam Steele]
(Photo by Steele and Company and British Library Digital Collections, HS85/10/11347. License: Public Domain)

2–19. Mary Ann Shadd [Cary] (1850s). An African American abolitionist, educator, lawyer, and writer.
(Photo by Unknown Author and nps.gov, courtesy of National Archives of Canada, C-029977. License: Public Domain)

Major-General Sir Isaac Brock

In July 1812, Major-General Sir Isaac Brock captured Detroit but was killed while defending against an American attack at Queenston Heights, near Niagara Falls, a battle the Americans lost.

Major-General Robert Ross

In retaliation to the Americans burning Government House and the Parliament Buildings in York (now Toronto) in 1813, Major-General Robert Ross led an expedition from Nova Scotia in 1814 that burned down the White House and other public buildings in Washington, D.C. He died in battle soon afterwards and was buried in Halifax with full military honours.

Major-General Sir Sam Steele

One of Canada's most colourful heroes, Major-General Sir Sam Steele came from the ranks of the Royal Canadian Mounted Police (RCMP or "the Mounties") and was a solider of the Queen. He is a great frontier hero and Mounted Policeman.

Marjorie Turner-Bailey

Marjorie Turner-Bailey is an Olympian of Nova Scotia and a descendant of black Loyalists (escaped slaves and freed men and women of African origin who in the 1780s fled to Canada from America, where slavery remained legal until 1863).

Martin Frobisher

English explorer, Martin Frobisher penetrated the uncharted Arctic for Queen Elizabeth I in 1576. Nunavut capital Iqaluit was formerly Frobisher Bay, named after Martin Frobisher.

Mary Ann Shadd Cary

An outspoken activist in the movement to abolish slavery in the U.S.A., Mary Ann Shadd Cary, in 1853, became the first woman publisher in Canada and helped to found and edit The Provincial Freeman, a weekly newspaper dedicated to anti-slavery. She helped black immigration to Canada and temperance (urging people to drink less alcohol), and upholding British rule.

The Métis

A distinct people of mixed Aboriginal and European ancestry, the majority of the Métis live in the Prairie provinces. They come from both French-speaking and English-speaking backgrounds, and speak their own dialect, Michif. About 30% of the Aboriginal people are Métis.

2-20. Oscar Peterson and Niels-Henning Ørsted Pedersen in Hamburg.
(Photo by Heinrich Klaffs. © 2010. License: Attribution-ShareAlike 2.0 Generic (CC BY-SA 2.0).
https://commons.wikimedia.org/wiki/File:Peterson_and_%C3%98rsted_in_Hamburg.jpg)

The North West Mounted Police (NWMP)

The North West Mounted Police (NWMP) founded Fort Calgary, Fort MacLeod and other centres that are cities and towns today. Regina became the NWMP headquarters.

Orville Fisher

A painter, Orville Fisher depicted the epic invasion of Normandy (known as D-Day) in northern France on June 6, 1944. He painted the moment when about 15,000 Canadian troops stormed and captured Juno Beach from the German Army, a great national achievement.

Oscar Peterson

Jazz pianist Oscar Peterson received the Order of Canada from Roland Michener, the 20th Governor General in 1973.

Paul Henderson

In 1972, Paul Henderson scored the winning goal for Canada in the Canada-Soviet Summit Series. This goal is often referred to as "the goal heard around the world" and is still remembered today as an important event in both sports and cultural history.

Phil Edwards

A Canadian track and field champion, Phil Edwards was born in British Guiana. He won bronze medals for Canada in the 1928, 1932 and 1936 Olympics. Edwards served as a captain in the Canadian Army during the Second World War. He graduated from McGill University Medical School, worked as a Montreal doctor, and became an expert in tropical diseases.

Pierre de Monts

In 1604, the first European settlement north of Florida was established by French explorers Pierre de Monts and Samuel de Champlain, first on St. Croix Island (in present-day Maine), then at port-Royal in Acadia (present-day Nova Scotia).

Pierre Le Moyne, Sieur d'Iberville

A great hero of New France (Quebec), Pierre Le Moyne, Sieur d'Iberville won many victories over the English, from James Bay in the north to Nevis in the Caribbean, in the late 17th and early 18th centuries.

Quebecers

Quebecers (Québécois) are the people of Quebec, the vast majority French-speaking. Most are descendants of about 8,500 French settlers from the 1600s and 1700s and maintain a unique identity, culture and language. Around one (1) million Anglo-Quebecers have a heritage of over 250 years and form a vibrant part of the Quebec fabric. The House of Commons recognized in 2006 that the Québécois form a nation within a united Canada.

2–21. Canada's sons and Great Britain in the world war (circa 1919). [General Sir Arthur Currie]
(Photo by George Gallie Nasmith; Toronto, The John C. Winston co., Limited; and The Library of Congress. License: CC0 1.0 Universal (CC0 1.0) Public Domain Dedication)

Queen Elizabeth II

Queen Elizabeth II has been Queen of Canada since 1952. Her Majesty opened the 23rd Parliament (1957). Her Majesty marked her Golden Jubilee in 2002, celebrated her Diamond Jubilee (60 years as Sovereign) in 2012, and celebrated her Platinum Jubilee (70 years as Sovereign) in 2022. Queen Victoria is her great-great-grandmother.

Robert Baldwin, Sir Louis-Hippolyte La Fontaine and Joseph Howe

Reformers Robert Baldwin and Sir Louis-Hippolyte La Fontaine, in parallel with Joseph Howe in Nova Scotia, worked with British governors toward responsible government.

Roland Michener

The 20th Governor General was Roland Michener.

Samuel de Champlain

In 1604, French explorer Samuel de Champlain helped establish the first European settlement north of Florida along with fellow explorer Pierre de Monts, first on St. Croix Island (Maine), then port-Royal in Acadia (Nova Scotia). In 1608, Champlain built a fortress at what is now Québec City. He allied the colony with the Algonquin, Montagnais and Huron (historic enemies of the Iroquois), a confederation of First Nations who battled with the French settlements for a century.

Sir Arthur Currie

A reserve officer, General Sir Arthur Currie became Canada's greatest soldier. In 1918, under his command, the Canadian Corps advanced alongside the French and British Empire troops in the last hundred days. These included the victorious

Battle of Amiens on August 8, 1918–which the Germans called "the black day of the German Army"–followed by Arras, Canal du Nord, Cambrai and Mons.

*Sir Étienne-Paschal Taché
and Sir George-Étienne Cartier*

Reformers Sir Étienne-Paschal Taché and Sir George-Étienne Cartier later became Fathers of Confederation.

Sir George-Étienne Cartier

The key architect of Confederation, Sir George-Étienne Cartier was a close ally of Sir John Alexander Macdonald. Cartier was a patriotic Canadien (a French-Canadian from Quebec), and led Quebec into Confederation. He helped negotiate the entry of the Northwest Territories, Manitoba, and British Columbia into Canada.

Sir Guy Carleton (Lord Dorchester)

As Governor of Quebec, Sir Guy Carleton (Lord Dorchester) defended the rights of the Canadiens (French-Canadians from Quebec). He defeated an American military invasion of Quebec in 1775, and supervised the Loyalist migration to Nova Scotia and Quebec (1782–1783).

Sir John Alexander Macdonald

Sir John Alexander Macdonald came to Upper Canada (later Ontario) as a child. In 1867, he was a Father of Confederation, and became Canada's first Prime Minister. After the first Métis uprising, in 1873, Macdonald established the North West Mounted Police (NWMP) to pacify the West and assist in negotiations with the Indians. January 11 is recognized as Sir John A. Macdonald Day and his portrait is on the Canadian $10 bill.

2–22. Sir John A. Macdonald (circa 1875).
[1st Prime Minister of Canada]
(Photo by George Lancefield. License: Public Domain)

Sir Leonard Tilley

Elected official Sir Leonard Tilley was a Father of Confederation from New Brunswick and, in 1864, suggested the term Dominion of Canada. He was inspired by Psalm 72 in the Bible which refers to "dominion from sea to sea and from the river to the ends of the earth." This phrase embodied the vision of building a powerful, united, wealthy and free country that spanned a continent. The title Dominion from Sea to Sea was written into the Constitution, and used officially for about 100 years. This title remains part of Canada's heritage today.

Sir Louis-Hippolyte La Fontaine

A reformer, Sir Louis-Hippolyte La Fontaine worked with British governors toward responsible government, and was a champion of democracy and French language rights. In 1849, he became the first (head) leader of a responsible government (similar to a prime minister) in Canada.

Sir Robert Borden

In 1917, the federal government of Sir Robert Borden gave women the right to vote in federal elections — first to nurses at the battle front, then to women who were related to men in active wartime service — thanks to the leadership of women (Dr. Emily Stowe) and other suffragettes.

Sir Wilfrid Laurier

Since Confederation, Sir Wilfrid Laurier became the first French-Canadian prime minister, and encouraged immigration to the West. His portrait is on the Canadian $5 bill.

Sir William Logan

A world-famous geologist, Sir William Logan (born in Montreal in 1798 to Scottish immigrant parents) is considered one of Canada's greatest scientists. He founded and directed the Geological Survey of Canada from 1842 to 1869. Mount Logan is named in his honour.

Vincent Massey

The 18th Governor General was Vincent Massey.

2–23. Sir Louis-Hippolyte La Fontaine.
(Photo by William Notman. License: Public Domain)

2–24. The Rt. Hon. Sir Robert Laird Borden, March 1918.
(Photo by William James Topley. Library and Archives Canada, PA-027011. © 1918, 2005. License: Attribution 2.0 Generic (CC BY 2.0). https://www.flickr.com/photos/lac-bac/7196133434)

2–25. William E. Logan (1869), Canadian geologist.
(Photo by Unknown author. License: Public Domain)

TIMELINE
History of Canada

496	French King adopted the Fleur-de-Lys, the lily flower
1215	Magna Carta Signing in England (Great Charter of Freedoms)
1497	European exploration began in earnest with the expedition of John Cabot
1534 to 1542	Jacques Cartier made three voyages across the Atlantic, claiming land for King Francis I
1550s	Canada, the name, began appearing on maps
1576	Martin Frobisher penetrated the uncharted Arctic for Queen Elizabeth I
1600s to 1700s	Quebecers maintained a unique identity, culture and language
	First European Settlement North of Florida (1604)
1604	First on St. Croix Island (Maine), then at port-Royal in Acadia (Nova Scotia)
1608	Samuel de Champlain built a fortress at what is now Québec City
1610	English settlement began
1690	Count Frontenac refused to surrender Quebec to the English
1700s	France and Great Britain battled for control of North America
1701	The French and the Iroquois made peace
1755 to 1763	**The "Great Upheaval"** The Acadians were deported from their homeland during the Britain and France war

Canada History

History of Canada

1800s to 1980s	The federal government placed Aboriginal children in residential schools
1805	Defeat of Napoleon Bonaparte's fleet in the Battle of Trafalgar
1807	The British Parliament prohibited the buying and selling of slaves
1812	**War of 1812: The Fight for Canada** — United States launched an invasion June 1812, believing it would conquer Canada
1813	Americans burned Government House and the Parliament Buildings in York (now Toronto)
1814	Major-General Robert Ross led an expedition that burned down the White House
1815	The Duke of Wellington defeated Napoleon
1830s	Some reformers believed Canada should adopt American republican values, join the U.S.
1832	The Montreal Stock Exchange opened
1833	The British Parliament abolished slavery throughout the Empire
1837 to 1838	Armed rebellions occurred outside Montreal and in Toronto and were defeated
1840	Upper and Lower Canada were united as the Province of Canada
1842 to 1869	Sir William Logan founded and directed the Geological Survey of Canada
1847 to 1848	The first British North American colony to attain full responsible government was Nova Scotia

Canada History

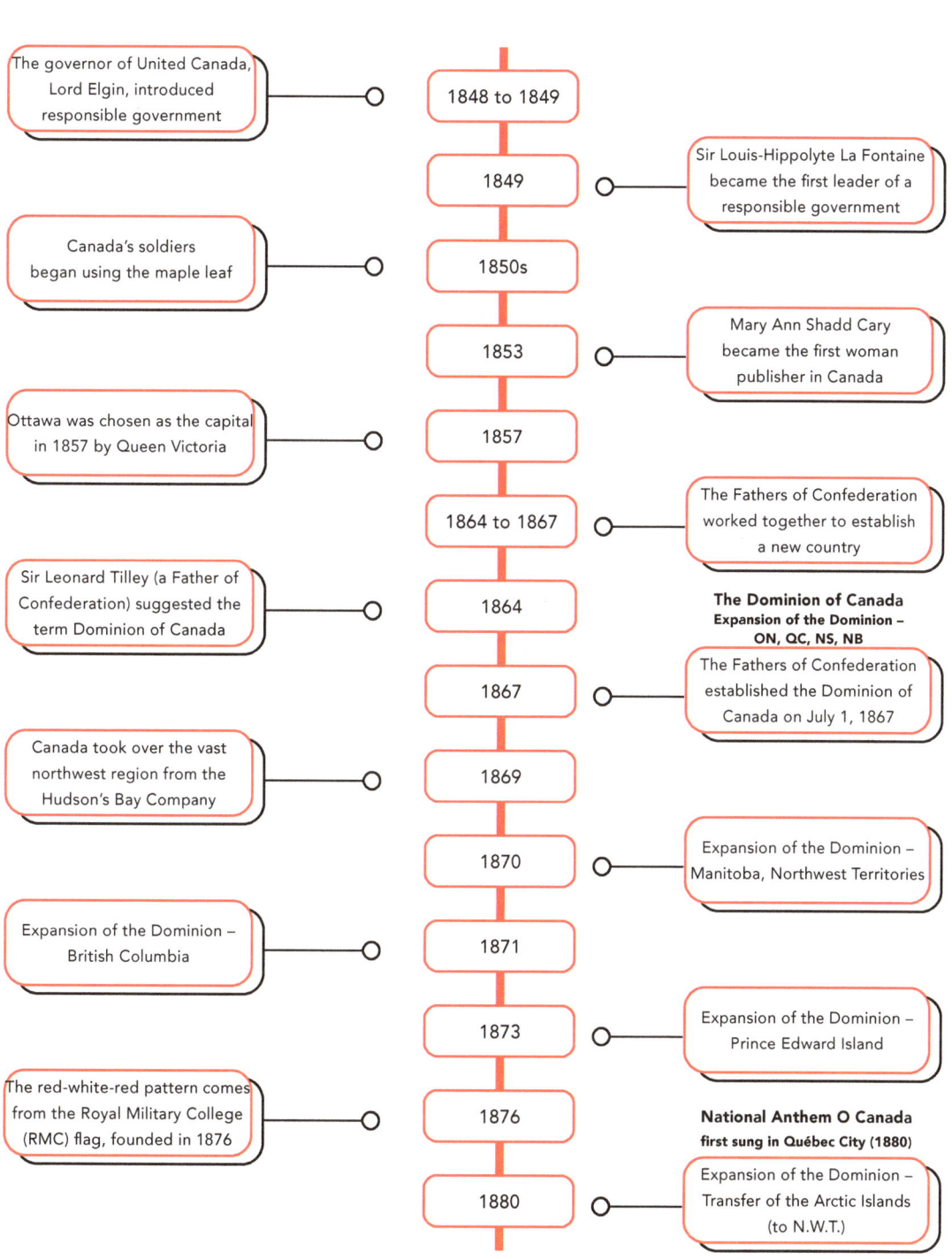

1848 to 1849	The governor of United Canada, Lord Elgin, introduced responsible government
1849	Sir Louis-Hippolyte La Fontaine became the first leader of a responsible government
1850s	Canada's soldiers began using the maple leaf
1853	Mary Ann Shadd Cary became the first woman publisher in Canada
1857	Ottawa was chosen as the capital in 1857 by Queen Victoria
1864 to 1867	The Fathers of Confederation worked together to establish a new country
1864	Sir Leonard Tilley (a Father of Confederation) suggested the term Dominion of Canada. **The Dominion of Canada** Expansion of the Dominion – ON, QC, NS, NB
1867	The Fathers of Confederation established the Dominion of Canada on July 1, 1867
1869	Canada took over the vast northwest region from the Hudson's Bay Company
1870	Expansion of the Dominion – Manitoba, Northwest Territories
1871	Expansion of the Dominion – British Columbia
1873	Expansion of the Dominion – Prince Edward Island
1876	The red-white-red pattern comes from the Royal Military College (RMC) flag, founded in 1876. **National Anthem O Canada** first sung in Québec City (1880)
1880	Expansion of the Dominion – Transfer of the Arctic Islands (to N.W.T.)

History of Canada

1885	Donald Smith drove the last spike of the Canadian Pacific Railway on November 7, 1885
1890s	Thousands of miners came to the Yukon during the Gold Rush of the 1890s
1891	Basketball was invented by Canadian James Naismith
1892	The National Hockey League plays for the championship Stanley Cup
1898	Expansion of the Dominion – Yukon Territory
1899 to 1902	Over 7,000 volunteered to fight in the South African War, known as the Boer War
1900s	Canada's economy grew and became more industrialized during the economic boom
1900	Canadians joined the battles of Paardeberg ("Horse Mountain") and Lillefontein
1905	Expansion of the Dominion – Alberta, Saskatchewan
1909	**Canadian Football League (CFL)** Governor General Lord Grey donated the championship Grey Cup for teams competing
1914	Ottawa formed the Canadian Expeditionary Force (later the Canadian Corps)
1914 to 1920	Ottawa interned former Austro-Hungarians as "enemy aliens" in labour camps across Canada
1916	Manitoba became the first province to grant voting rights to women
1917	The Canadian Corps captured Vimy Ridge in April 1917

Canada History

Battle of Amiens - August 8, 1918

- 1918 — Canadian Corps advanced alongside the French and British Empire troops
- 1920s — Some believed that the British West Indies should become part of Canada
- 1920 — Group of Seven was founded, painted in a style that captured rugged wilderness landscapes
- 1921 — King George V assigned Canada's national colours (white and red)
- 1923 — King George V was on the Dominion of Canada $1 bill
- 1927 — Old Age Security was devised as early as 1927
- 1928 — Phil Edwards won bronze medals for Canada in the 1928 Olympics
- 1929 — The stock market crash of 1929 led to the Great Depression known as the "Dirty Thirties"
- 1932 — Phil Edwards won bronze medals for Canada in the 1932 Olympics
- 1933 — Unemployment reached 27% and many businesses were wiped out
- 1934 — The Bank of Canada was created to manage the money supply, stabilize the financial system
- 1935 to 1940 — John Buchan was a popular 15th Governor General of Canada
- 1936 — Phil Edwards won bronze medals for Canada in the 1936 Olympics
- 1939 — Immigration dropped and many refugees turned away, including Jews fleeing Nazi Germany

History of Canada

- **1940** — Women granted the right to vote in Quebec
- **1941** — **Imperial Japan Attack**: Canadians fought bravely, suffered losses in unsuccessful defence of Hong Kong
- **1942** — **On the Coast of France**: Canadians fought bravely, suffered losses in failed raid on Nazi-controlled Dieppe
- **1943 to 1944** — Canadians took part in the liberation of Italy
- **1944** — **D-Day Invasion, June 6, 1944**: Canadians captured Juno Beach in World War II, part of the Allied invasion of Normandy
- **1944 to 1945** — The Canadian Army liberated the Netherlands
- **1945** — Canadian Army helped force the German surrender in Europe May 8, 1945
- **1945 to 1970** — Canada enjoyed one of the strongest economies among industrialized nations
- **1947** — Discovery of oil in Alberta began Canada's modern energy industry
- **1948** — Quebec adopted its own flag, based on the Cross and the Fleur-de-Lys
- **1949** — Expansion of the Dominion – Newfoundland and Labrador
- **1950s** — The Les Automatistes of Quebec were pioneers of modern abstract art
- **1950 to 1953** — Canada participated in the UN operation defending South Korea in the Korean War
- **1951** — For the first time, a majority of Canadians could afford adequate food, shelter and clothing

Canada History

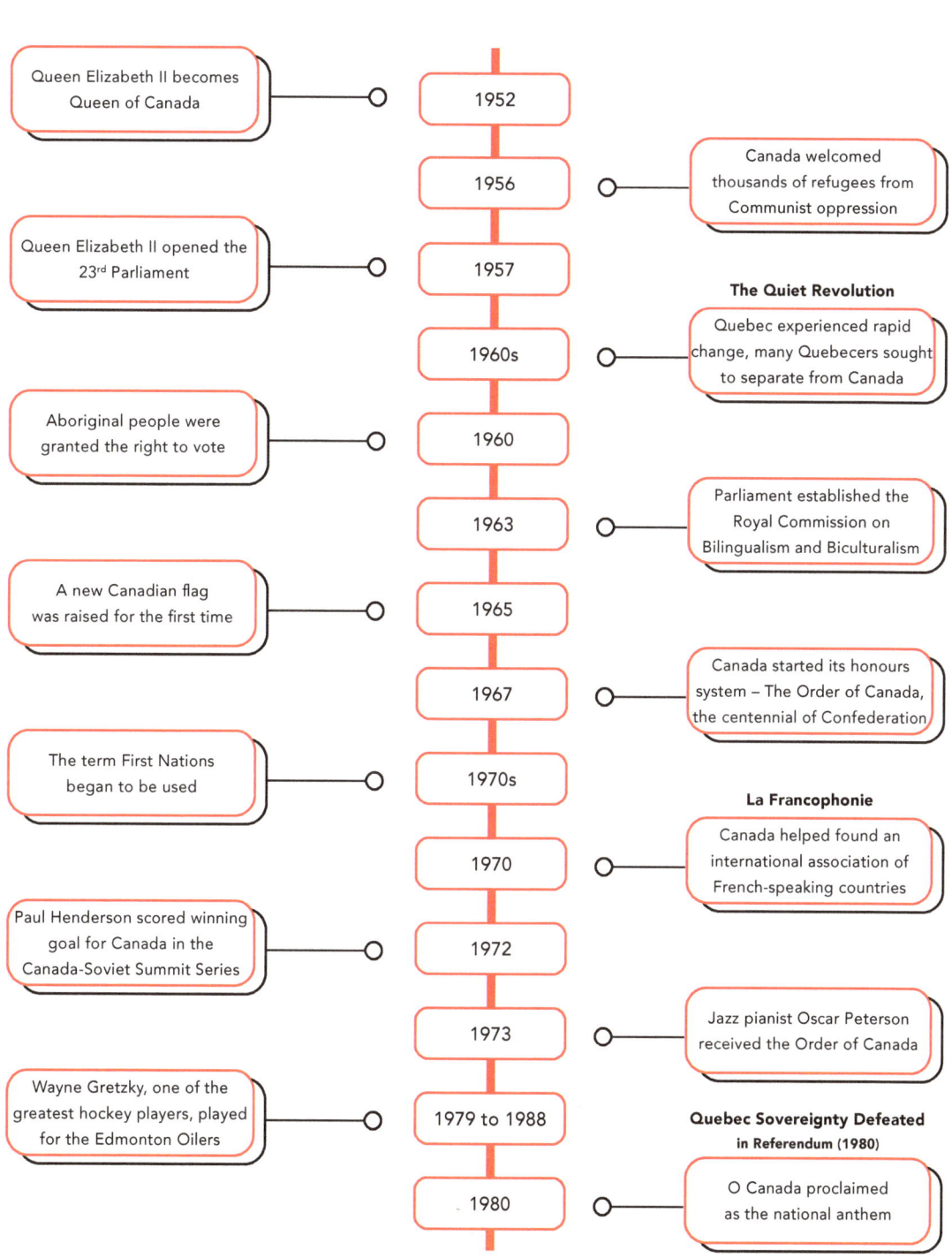

1952	Queen Elizabeth II becomes Queen of Canada
1956	Canada welcomed thousands of refugees from Communist oppression
1957	Queen Elizabeth II opened the 23rd Parliament
1960s	**The Quiet Revolution** — Quebec experienced rapid change, many Quebecers sought to separate from Canada
1960	Aboriginal people were granted the right to vote
1963	Parliament established the Royal Commission on Bilingualism and Biculturalism
1965	A new Canadian flag was raised for the first time
1967	Canada started its honours system – The Order of Canada, the centennial of Confederation
1970s	The term First Nations began to be used
1970	**La Francophonie** — Canada helped found an international association of French-speaking countries
1972	Paul Henderson scored winning goal for Canada in the Canada-Soviet Summit Series
1973	Jazz pianist Oscar Peterson received the Order of Canada
1979 to 1988	Wayne Gretzky, one of the greatest hockey players, played for the Edmonton Oilers. **Quebec Sovereignty Defeated in Referendum (1980)**
1980	O Canada proclaimed as the national anthem

History of Canada

- **1982** — Constitution of Canada amended to establish the Canadian Charter of Rights and Freedoms
- **1985** — Rick Hansen circled the globe in a wheelchair to raise funds for spinal cord research
- **1988** — **Wartime Wrongs** Government of Canada apologized and compensated Canadian Japanese victims
- **1994** — Mexico became a partner in the broader North American Free Trade Agreement (NAFTA)
- **1995** — Quebec's sovereignty was again defeated in a second referendum, the first in 1980
- **1996** — **Olympic Summer Games** Donovan Bailey became a world record sprinter and double Olympic gold medallist
- **1999** — Expansion of the Dominion – Nunavut
- **2002** — **Olympic Winter Games** Catriona Le May Doan carried the flag after winning a gold medal in speed skating
- **2005** — The Clarkson Cup, established by Adrienne Clarkson, is awarded for women's hockey
- **2006** — Government of Canada apologized to the Chinese for Head Tax discriminatory policy
- **2008** — Ottawa formally apologized to the former Aboriginal students
- **2010** — Team Canada won gold in men's hockey at the Winter Olympics in Vancouver
- **Today** — Canada remains a leading member of the Commonwealth, with other states of the Empire

03 Canada Geography

3-1. Dominion of Canada.
(Photo by University of British Columbia (UBC) Library. License: Public Domain)

The old Province of Canada was split into two new provinces: Ontario and Quebec, and together with New Brunswick and Nova Scotia formed the new country the Dominion of Canada.

Canada is the second largest country on earth—about 10 million square kilometres. Three oceans line Canada's frontiers: the Pacific Ocean in the west, Atlantic Ocean in the east, and Arctic Ocean to the north. Along the southern edge of Canada lies the Canada-United States boundary. Both Canada and the U.S.A. are committed to a safe, secure and efficient frontier. The Rideau Canal, once a military waterway in Ottawa, part of a network of forts preventing the U.S.A. from invading Canada again, is now a tourist attraction and winter skate-way. At Blaine, in the State of Washington, the Peace Arch, inscribed with the words "children of a common mother" and "brethren dwelling together in unity," symbolizes Canada's close ties and common interests with the U.S.A.

Canada has a population of about 34 million people. While the majority live in cities, Canadians also live in small towns, rural areas and everywhere in between. Canadians have built a prosperous society in a rugged environment from Canada's Atlantic shores to the Pacific Ocean and to the Arctic Circle. The Atlantic colonies and the two Canadas were known collectively as British North America.

Canada is often referred to as a "land of immigrants" because, over the past 200 years, millions of newcomers have helped to build and defend Canada's way of life. The largest ethnic groups are the English, French, Scottish, Irish, German, Italian, Chinese, Aboriginal, Ukrainian, Dutch, South Asian, and Scandinavian. About 65% of the Aboriginal people are First Nations, 30% of the Aboriginal people are Métis, and about 4% of the Aboriginal people are Inuit.

3–2. The British colonies in North America.
(Photo by Engraver Faden William. © 1777. License: Attribution 4.0 International (CC BY 4.0). https://commons.wikimedia.org/wiki/File:The_British_colonies_in_North_America.jpg)

3–3. Canada's Regions, Provinces/Territories, and Capital Cities.
(Photo by Citizenship and Immigration Canada. © 2012, 2017. Discover Canada)

While the majority of Francophones live in the province of Quebec, about one (1) million Francophones live in Ontario, New Brunswick and Manitoba, with a smaller presence in other provinces. New Brunswick is the only officially bilingual province. Quebecers are the people of Quebec, the vast majority French-speaking. Non-official languages are widely spoken in Canadian homes. Chinese languages are the second most-spoken at home, after English, in two of Canada's biggest cities.

The great majority of Canadians identify as Christians. The largest religious affiliation is Catholic, followed by various Protestant churches.

Canada's diversity includes gay and lesbian Canadians, who enjoy the full protection of and equal treatment under the law, including access to civil marriage.

Regions of Canada

Canada includes five (5) distinct regions: The Atlantic Provinces, Central Canada, Prairie Provinces, West Coast, and Northern Territories.

The National Capital - Ottawa, located on the Ottawa River, was chosen as the capital in 1857 by Queen Victoria, the great-great-grandmother of Queen Elizabeth II. Today it is Canada's fourth largest metropolitan area. The National Capital Region preserves and enhances the historical and cultural heritage and natural environment. Ottawa is the Capital of Canada.

Provinces and Territories

Canada has ten (10) provinces and three (3) territories. Each province and territory has its own capital city.

Atlantic Provinces

Atlantic Canada's coasts and natural resources, including fishing, farming, forestry and mining, have made these provinces an important part of Canada's history and development. The Atlantic Ocean brings cool winters and cool humid summers.

Newfoundland and Labrador (Capital City: St. John's)

The most easterly point in North America is Newfoundland and Labrador and has its own time zone. In addition to its natural beauty, the province has a unique heritage linked to the sea. The oldest colony of the British Empire and a strategic prize in Canada's early history, the province has long been known for its fisheries, coastal fishing villages and distinct culture. Today off-shore oil and gas extraction contributes a substantial part of the economy. Labrador also has immense hydro-electric resources.

Prince Edward Island (Capital City: Charlottetown)

The smallest province is Prince Edward Island (P.E.I.), known for its beaches, red soil and agriculture, especially potatoes. P.E.I. is the birthplace of Confederation, connected to mainland Canada by one of the longest continuous multi-span bridges in the world, the Confederation Bridge. Anne of Green Gables, set in P.E.I. by Lucy Maud Montgomery, is a much-loved story about the adventures of a little red-headed orphan girl.

Nova Scotia (Capital City: Halifax)

The most populous Atlantic Province is Nova Scotia. With a rich history as the gateway to Canada and known for the world's highest tides in the Bay of Fundy, Nova Scotia's identity is linked to shipbuilding, fisheries and shipping. As Canada's largest east coast port, the capital Halifax has played an important role in Atlantic trade and defence and is home to Canada's largest naval base. The province has a long history of coal mining, forestry and agriculture. Today there is also off-shore oil and gas exploration. The province's Celtic and Gaelic traditions sustain a vibrant culture.

New Brunswick (Capital City: Fredericton)

Situated in the Appalachian Range, New Brunswick was founded by the United Empire Loyalists. The St. John River system in the province has the second largest river system on North America's Atlantic coastline. Forestry, agriculture, fisheries, mining, food processing and tourism are the principal industries. Saint John is the largest city, port and manufacturing centre. Moncton is the principal Francophone Acadian centre. Fredericton, is the historic capital. New Brunswick is the only officially bilingual province, about one-third of the population lives and works in French. The province's pioneer Loyalist, French cultural heritage and history come alive in street festivals and traditional music.

3–4. Central Canada.
(Photo by Connormah. © 2009.
License: Attribution 3.0 Unported (CC BY 3.0).
https://commons.wikimedia.org/)/wiki/File:Central_Canada.svg)

Central Canada

More than half the people in Canada live in cities and towns near the Great Lakes and the St. Lawrence River in southern Quebec and Ontario, known as Central Canada (the industrial and manufacturing heartland). Southern Ontario and Quebec have cold winters and warm humid summers. Together, Ontario and Quebec produce more than three-quarters of all Canadian manufactured goods.

3–5. Quebec in Canada.
(Photo by MapGrid. © 2020. License: Attribution-ShareAlike 4.0 International (CC BY-SA 4.0).
https://commons.wikimedia.org/wiki/File:Quebec_in_Canada_2.svg)

Quebec (Capital City: Québec City)

Nearly eight (8) million people live in Quebec. The vast majority of people live in Quebec along or near the St. Lawrence River. More than three-quarters speak French as their first language. The resources of the Canadian Shield have helped Quebec to develop important industries, including forestry, energy and mining. Quebec is Canada's main producer of pulp and paper. The province's huge supply of fresh water has made it Canada's largest producer of hydro electricity. Quebecers are leaders in cutting-edge industries such as pharmaceuticals and aeronautics. Quebec films, music, literary works and food have international stature, especially in La Francophonie, an association of French-speaking nations. Montreal, Canada's second largest city and the second largest mainly French-speaking city in the world after Paris, is famous for its cultural diversity.

3–6. Ontario in Canada.
(Photo by MapGrid. © 2020. License: Attribution-ShareAlike 4.0 International (CC BY-SA 4.0).
https://commons.wikimedia.org/wiki/File:Ontario_in_Canada_2.svg)

Ontario (Capital City: Toronto)

At more than 12 million, the people of Ontario make up more than one-third of Canadians. The large and culturally diverse population, natural resources and strategic location contribute to a vital economy. Toronto is the largest city in Canada and the country's main financial centre. Many people work in the service or manufacturing industries, which produce a large percentage of Canada's exports. The Niagara region is known for its vineyards, wines and fruit crops. Ontario farmers raise dairy and beef cattle, poultry, and vegetable and grain crops. Founded by United Empire Loyalists, Ontario also has the largest French speaking population outside of Quebec, with a proud history of preserving their language and culture. There are five Great Lakes located between Ontario and the United States: Lake Ontario, Lake Erie, Lake Huron, Lake Michigan (in the U.S.A.) and Lake Superior, the largest freshwater lake in the world.

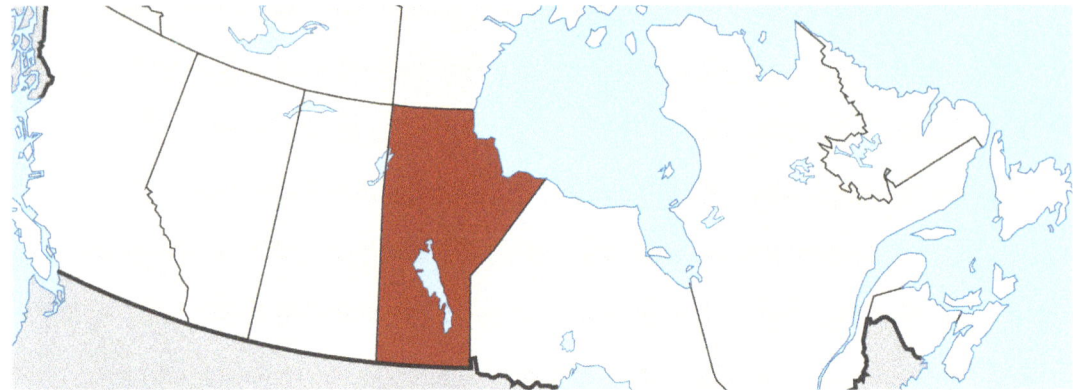

3–7. Manitoba in Canada.
(Photo by Wikimedia Commons. © 2011. License: Attribution-ShareAlike 2.5 Generic (CC BY-SA 2.5).
https://commons.wikimedia.org/wiki/File:Manitoba_in_Canada.svg)

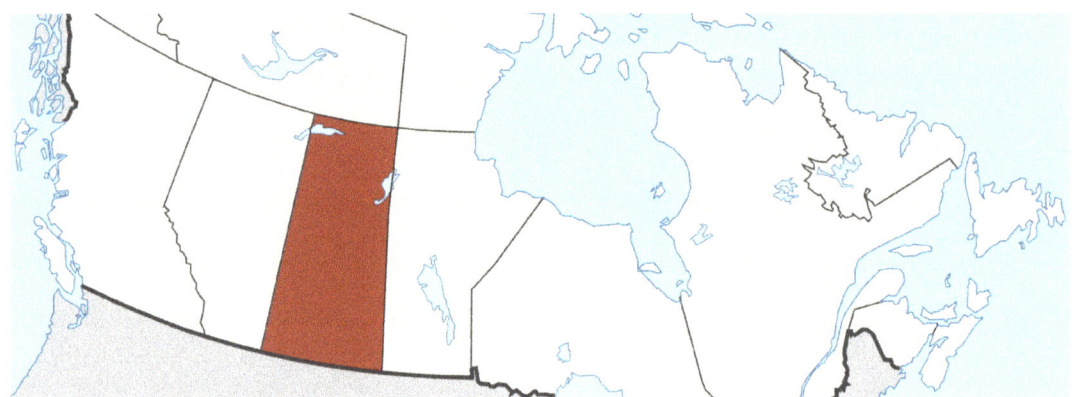

3–8. Saskatchewan in Canada.
(Photo by Wikimedia Commons. © 2011. License: Attribution-ShareAlike 2.5 Generic (CC BY-SA 2.5).
https://commons.wikimedia.org/wiki/File:Saskatchewan_in_Canada.svg)

3–9. Alberta in Canada.
(Photo by MapGrid. © 2020. License: Attribution-ShareAlike 4.0 International (CC BY-SA 4.0).
https://commons.wikimedia.org/wiki/File:Alberta_in_Canada_2.svg)

3–10. Canada Prairie provinces map.
(Photo by Derfel73 and Lokal Profil. © 2011.
License: Attribution-ShareAlike 3.0 Unported (CC BY-SA 3.0). https://commons.wikimedia.org/wiki/File:Canada_Prairie_provinces_map.svg)

Prairie Provinces

Manitoba, Saskatchewan and Alberta are the Prairie Provinces, rich in energy resources and some of the most fertile farmland in the world. The region is mostly dry, with cold winters and hot summers.

Manitoba (Capital City: Winnipeg)

Manitoba's economy is based on agriculture, mining and hydro-electric power generation. The province's most populous city is Winnipeg, whose Exchange District includes the most famous street intersection in Canada, Portage and Main. Winnipeg's French Quarter, St. Boniface, has Western Canada's largest Francophone community at about 45,000. Manitoba is also an important centre of Ukrainian culture, with around 14% reporting Ukrainian origins, and the largest Aboriginal population of any province, at over 15%.

Saskatchewan (Capital City: Regina)

Saskatchewan, once known as the "breadbasket of the world" and the "wheat province," has about 40% of the arable land in Canada and is the country's largest producer of grains and oilseeds. It also boasts the world's richest deposits of uranium and potash, used in fertilizer, and produces oil and natural gas. Regina, the capital, is home to the training academy of the Royal Canadian Mounted Police. Saskatoon, the largest city, is the headquarters of the mining industry and an important educational, research and technology centre.

Alberta (Capital City: Edmonton)

Alberta is the most populous Prairie province. The province, and the world-famous Lake Louise in the Rocky Mountains, were both named after Princess Louise Caroline Alberta, fourth daughter of Queen Victoria. Alberta has five (5) national parks, including Banff National Park, established in 1885. The rugged Badlands house some of the world's richest deposits of prehistoric fossils and

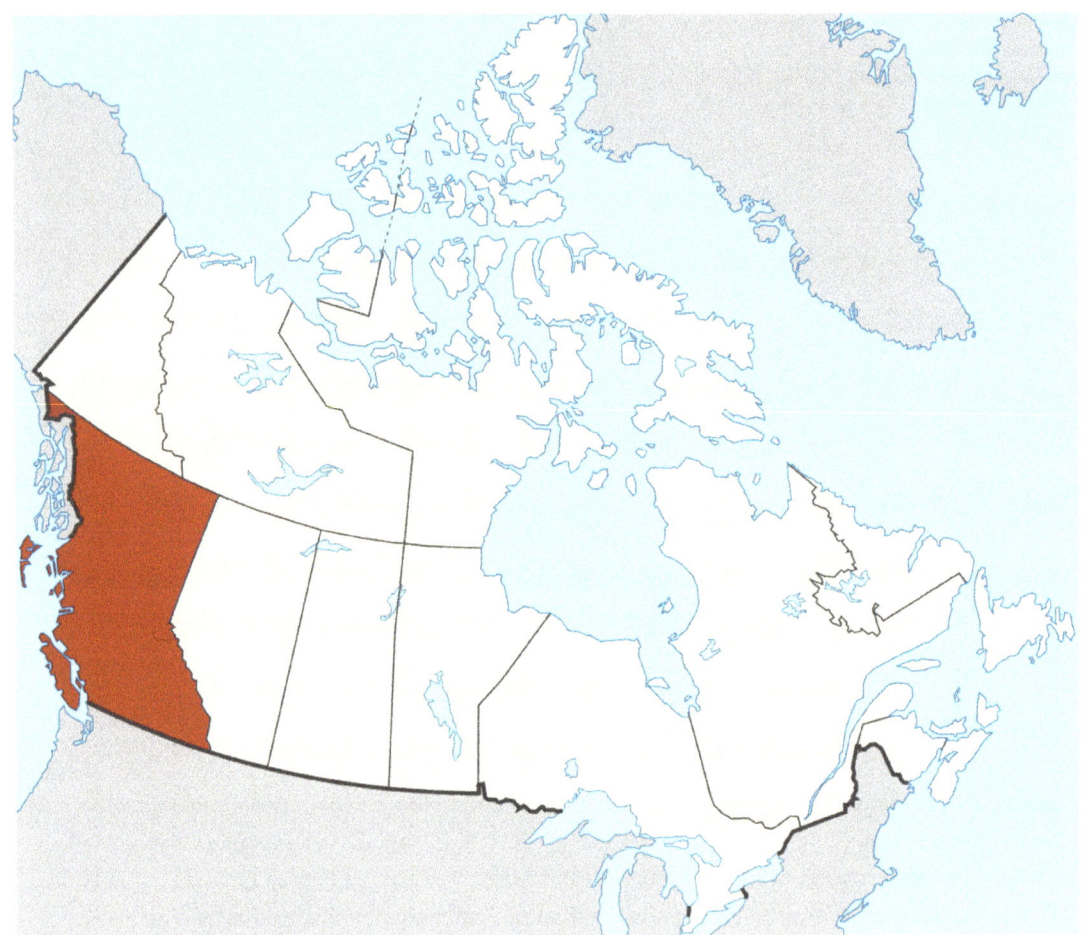

3–11. British Columbia in Canada.
(Photo by Allice Hunter. © 2017. License: Attribution-ShareAlike 4.0 International (CC BY-SA 4.0).
https://commons.wikimedia.org/wiki/File:British_Columbia_highlighted_in_red_in_Canada.png)

3–12. Northern Territories in Canada.
(Photo by Allice Hunter. © 2021. License: Attribution-ShareAlike 4.0 International (CC BY-SA 4.0). https://commons.wikimedia.org/wiki/File:Northern_territories_in_Canada.svg)

dinosaur finds. Alberta is the largest producer of oil and gas, and the oil sands in the north are being developed as a major energy source. Alberta is also renowned for agriculture, especially for the vast cattle ranches that make Canada one of the world's major beef producers.

West Coast

British Columbia is known for its majestic mountains and as Canada's Pacific gateway. The Port of Vancouver, Canada's largest and busiest, handles billions of dollars in goods traded around the world. Warm airstreams from the Pacific Ocean give the B.C. coast a temperate climate.

British Columbia (Capital City: Victoria)

British Columbia (B.C.), on the Pacific coast, is Canada's westernmost province, with a population of about four (4) million. The Port of Vancouver is Canada's gateway to the Asia-Pacific. About one-half of all the goods produced in B.C. are forestry products, including lumber, newsprint, and pulp and paper products—the most valuable forestry industry in Canada. B.C. is also known for mining, fishing, and the fruit orchards and wine industry of the Okanagan Valley. B.C. has the most extensive park system in Canada, with approximately 600 provincial parks. The province's large Asian communities have made Chinese and Punjabi the most spoken languages in the cities after English. The capital, Victoria, is a tourist centre and headquarters of the navy's Pacific fleet.

North (The Northern Territories)

The Northwest Territories, Nunavut and Yukon contain about one-third of Canada's land mass. But have a population of about 100,000. There are gold, lead, copper, diamond and zinc mines. Oil and gas deposits are being developed. The North is often referred to as the "Land of the

3–13. Nunavut in Canada.
(Photo by André Akinyele. © 2022.
License: Attribution-ShareAlike 4.0 International (CC BY-SA 4.0).
https://creativecommons.org/licenses/by-sa/4.0/deed.en)

Midnight Sun" because at the height of summer, daylight can last up to 24 hours. In winter, the sun disappears and darkness sets in for three months. The Northern territories have long cold winters and short cool summers. Much of the North is made up of tundra, the vast rocky Arctic plain. There are no trees on the tundra because of the cold Arctic climate. The soil is permanently frozen because of the cold Arctic climate. Some continue to earn a living by hunting, fishing and trapping. Inuit art is sold throughout Canada and around the world.

Nunavut (Capital City: Iqaluit)

Meaning "our land" in Inukitut. Nunavut was established in 1999 from the eastern part of the Northwest Territories, including all of the former District of Keewatin. The capital is Iqaluit, formerly Frobisher Bay, named after the English explorer Martin Frobisher, who penetrated the uncharted Arctic for Queen Elizabeth I in 1576. The 19-member Legislative Assembly chooses a premier and ministers by consensus. Nunavut's population is about 85% Inuit. Inukitut is an official language. Inuktitut is the first language in schools.

Northwest Territories (Capital City: Yellowknife)

The Northwest Territories (N.W.T.) were originally made up in 1870 from Rupert's Land and the North-Western Territory. The capital Yellowknife is called the "diamond capital of North America." More than half the population is Aboriginal (Dene, Inuit and Métis). The Mackenzie River, at about 4,200 kilometres, is the second-longest river system in North America after the Mississippi.

3–14. Northwest Territories in Canada.
(Photo by André Akinyele. © 2022.
License: Attribution-ShareAlike 4.0 International (CC BY-SA 4.0).
https://creativecommons.org/licenses/by-sa/4.0/deed.en)

Yukon Territory (Capital City: Whitehorse)

Thousands of miners came to the Yukon during the Gold Rush of the 1890s, as celebrated in the poetry of Robert W. Service. Mining remains a significant part of the economy. The White Pass and Yukon Railway opened from Skagway in neighbouring Alaska to the territorial capital Whitehorse in 1900. The White Pass and Yukon Railway provides a spectacular tourist excursion across precipitous passes and bridges. Yukon holds the record for the coldest temperature ever recorded in Canada (-63°C / -81°F). Mount Logan, located in the Yukon, is the highest mountain in Canada and named in honour of Sir William Logan.

3–15. Yukon Territory in Canada.
(Photo by André Akinyele. © 2022.
License: Attribution-ShareAlike 4.0 International (CC BY-SA 4.0).
https://creativecommons.org/licenses/by-sa/4.0/deed.en)

TIMELINE
Geography of Canada

- **1604** — The Acadians, descendants of French colonists, began settling in the Maritime provinces
- **1791** — The Constitutional Act of 1791 divided the Province of Quebec into Upper and Lower Canada
- **1800s** — The majority of Canadians were born in Canada, true since the 1800s
- **1867** — The Dominion of Canada was officially born on July 1, 1867
- **1916** — Manitoba became the first province to grant voting rights to women
- **1940** — Due to the work of Thérèse Casgrain and others, Quebec granted women the vote
- **1970s** — Since the 1970s, most immigrants have come from Asian countries
- **Today** — **Partly an Outcome of The War of 1812 (Today)** — The Canada-U.S.A. Border ensures Canada remains independent of the U.S.

04   Canada Economy

4–1. Canadian money.
(Photo by Ptra / Canva)

Canada has always been a trading nation. The world's restrictive trading policies in the Depression era were opened up by such treaties as the General Agreement on Tariffs and Trade (GATT), now the World Trade Organization (WTO). Canada has the biggest bilateral trading relationship in the world and exports billions of dollars' worth of energy products, industrial goods, machinery, equipment, automotive, agricultural, fishing and forestry products, and consumer goods every year. Over three-quarters of Canadian exports are destined for the United States (U.S.A.), and Canada enjoys close relations with the U.S.A. Each is the other's largest trading partner, and integrated Canada-U.S.A. supply chains compete with the rest of the world. As Canadians, we could not maintain Canada's standard of living without engaging in trade with other nations. Commerce remains the engine of economic growth.

Formed during the French and British regimes, the first companies in Canada competed for the fur trade. Aboriginals and Europeans formed strong economic, religious and military bonds in the first 200 years of coexistence that laid the foundations of Canada. In the vast fur-trade economy, French and Aboriginal people collaborated, driven by the demand for beaver pelts in Europe. For centuries Canada's economy was based mainly on farming and on exporting natural resources such as fur, fish and timber, transported by roads, lakes, rivers, and canals. The first financial institutions opened in the late 18th and early 19th centuries. The Hudson's Bay Company, with French, British and Aboriginal employees, came to dominate the trade in the northwest from Fort Garry (Winnipeg) and Fort Edmonton to Fort Langley and Fort Victoria— trading posts that later became cities.

With prosperity for businesses and low unemployment, the "Roaring Twenties" were boom times, French-Canadian society and culture flourished in the postwar years. Postwar Canada enjoyed record prosperity and material progress. As prosperity grew, so did the ability to support social assistance programs. There was growing demand for the government to create a social safety net with minimum wages and a standard work week, and programs such as unemployment insurance.

Canada's Economy

Canada's Economy includes three (3) main types of industries: Service, Manufacturing, and Natural Resources. These industries have played an important part in the country's history and development.

Service Industries

Service industries provide thousands of different jobs in areas like transportation, education, health care, construction, banking, communications, retail services, tourism and government. More than 75% of working Canadians now have jobs in service industries.

Manufacturing Industries

Manufacturing industries make products to sell in Canada and around the world. Manufactured products include paper, high technology equipment, aerospace technology, automobiles, machinery, food, clothing and many other goods. Canada's largest international trading partner is the United States.

Natural Resources Industries

Natural resources industries include forestry, fishing, agriculture, mining and energy.

Canada's Services, Manufactured Goods, and Natural Resources

Canada's Financial Capital is Toronto's Business District. Toronto is the largest city in Canada and the country's main financial centre. Many people work in the service or manufacturing industries, which produce a large percentage of Canada's exports.

The Port of Vancouver, Canada's largest and busiest, handles billions of dollars in goods traded around the world. About one-half of all the goods produced in B.C. are forestry products, including lumber, newsprint, and pulp and paper products—the most valuable forestry industry in Canada. B.C. is also known for mining, fishing, and the fruit orchards and wine industry of the Okanagan Valley. B.C. has the most extensive park system in Canada, with approximately 600 provincial parks.

Alberta is the largest producer of oil and gas, and the oil sands in the north are being developed as a major energy source.

Manitoba's economy is based on agriculture, mining and hydro-electric power generation. The province's most populous city is Winnipeg, whose Exchange District includes the most famous street intersection in Canada, Portage and Main.

Saskatchewan is the country's largest producer of grains and oilseeds.

Central Canada (Ontario and Quebec) produce more than three-quarters of all Canadian manufactured goods. Quebec is Canada's main producer of pulp and paper. The Quebec province's huge supply of fresh water has made it Canada's largest producer of hydro-electricity.

Newfoundland and Labrador, today, produce off-shore oil, and its gas extraction contributes a substantial part of the economy. Labrador also has immense hydro-electric resources.

Halifax, Nova Scotia, as Canada's largest east coast port, has played an important role in Atlantic trade. Nova Scotia has a long history of coal mining, forestry and agriculture. Today, there is also off-shore oil and gas exploration.

TIMELINE
Economy of Canada

1832 — The Montreal Stock Exchange opened in 1832

1890s — **Economic Boom (1890s and early 1900s)** Canada's economy grew and became more industrialized

Before 1914 — **In the West Before 1914** The railway made it possible for immigrants to settle and develop a thriving agricultural sector

1920s — The "Roaring Twenties" were boom times – prosperity for businesses, low unemployment

1923 — King George V was on the Dominion of Canada $1 bill

1927 — Old Age Security was devised as early as 1927

1929 — The stock market crash of 1929 led to the Great Depression or the "Dirty Thirties"

1933 — Unemployment reached 27% and many businesses were wiped out

1934 — The Bank of Canada was created to manage the money supply and stabilize the financial system

1940 — Federal Government introduced unemployment insurance, now employment insurance

1945 to 1970 — Canada enjoyed one of the strongest economies among industrialized nations

1947 — The discovery of oil in Alberta began Canada's modern energy industry

1951 — A majority of Canadians were able to afford adequate food, shelter and clothing

1965 — The Canada and Quebec Pension Plans were devised

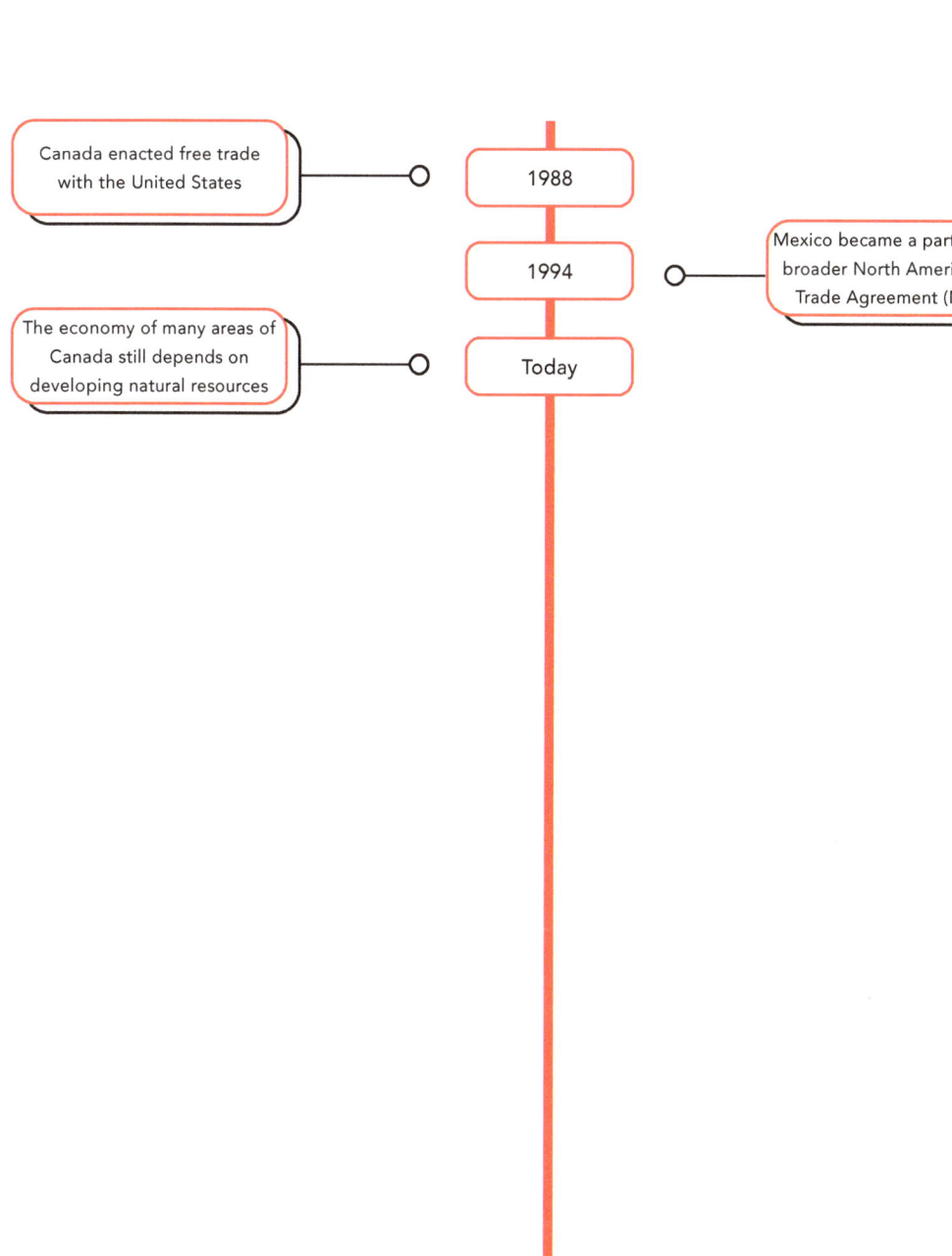

05   Canada Government

5–1. Statue of Robert Baldwin and Sir Louis-Hippolyte La Fontaine in Ottawa.
(Photo by Andrijko Z. © 2012. License: Attribution-ShareAlike 3.0 Unported (CC BY-SA 3.0). https://commons.wikimedia.org/wiki/File:Statue_of_Robert_Baldwin_and_Sir_Louis-Hippolyte_Lafontaine_in_Ottawa.JPG)

Responsible Government

Lord Durham recommended that Upper Canada (later Ontario) and Lower Canada (later Quebec) be merged and given responsible government. This meant that the ministers of the Crown must have the support of a majority of the elected representatives in order to govern.

In 1840, Upper Canada and Lower Canada were united as the Province of Canada. The first British North American colony to attain full responsible government was Nova Scotia in 1847–1848.

In 1848–1849 the governor of United Canada, Lord Elgin, with encouragement from London, introduced responsible government. This is the system that we have today: If the government loses a confidence vote in the assembly it must resign.

Reformers such as Sir Louis-Hippolyte La Fontaine and Robert Baldwin, in parallel with Joseph Howe in Nova Scotia, worked with British governors toward responsible government.

Sir Louis-Hippolyte La Fontaine, a champion of democracy and French language rights, became the first (head) leader of a responsible government (similar to a prime minister) in Canada in 1849.

Confederation

From 1864 to 1867, representatives of Nova Scotia, New Brunswick and the Province of Canada, with British support, worked together to establish a new country – these men are known as the Fathers of Confederation. The old Province of Canada was split into two new provinces: Ontario and Quebec,

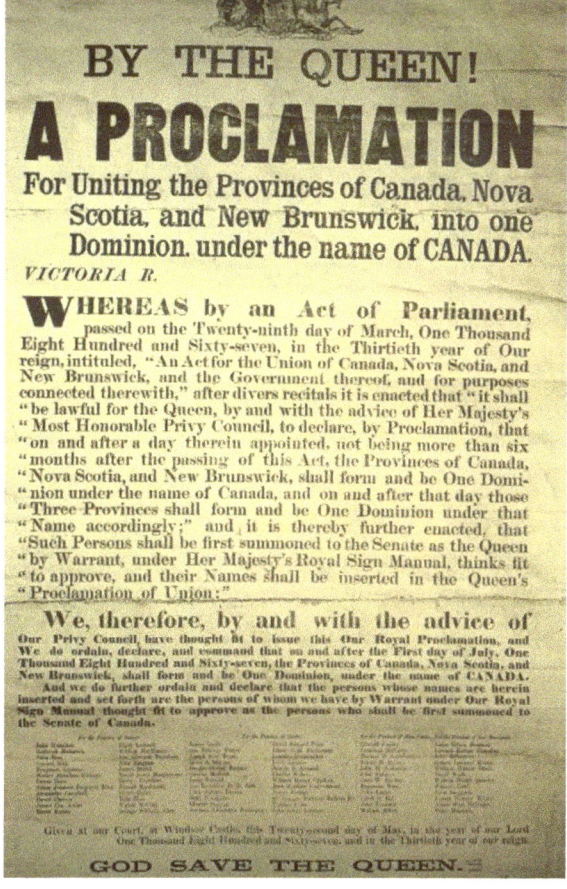

5–2. Proclamation of Canadian Confederation (1867).
(Photo by Royal Proclamation. License: Public Domain)

and together with New Brunswick and Nova Scotia formed the new country called the Dominion of Canada. Each province would elect its own legislature, have control of such areas as education and health.

The Fathers of Confederation established the Dominion of Canada on July 1, 1867, the birth of the country that we know today, and created two levels of government: Federal and Provincial.

Until 1982, July 1 was celebrated as "Dominion Day" to commemorate the day that Canada became a self-governing Dominion – today it is officially known as Canada Day. Sir Leonard Tilley, an elected official and a Father of Confederation from New Brunswick, suggested the term Dominion of Canada in 1864. He was inspired by Psalm 72 in the Bible which refers to "dominion from sea to sea and from the river to the ends of the earth." This phrase embodied the vision of building a powerful, united, wealthy and free country that spanned a continent.

5–3. Parliament Hill, Ottawa, Canada.
(Photo by Travelcoffeebook / Canva)

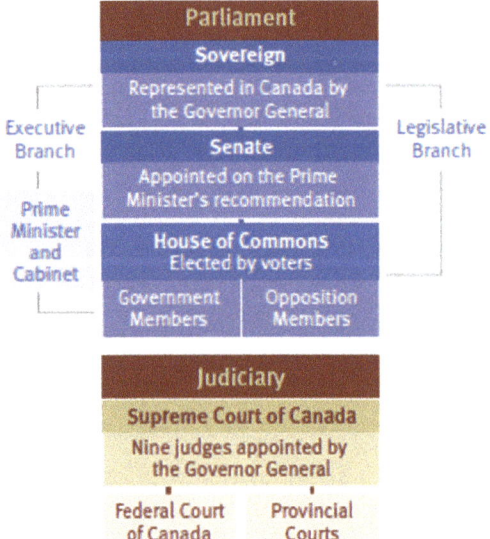

5–4. Canada system of government diagram.
(Photo by Citizenship and Immigration Canada. © 2012, 2017. Discover Canada)

The title Dominion from Sea to Sea was written into the Constitution, used officially for about 100 years, and remains part of Canada's heritage today.

The Canadian Crown

The Canadian Crown (The Crown) has been a symbol of the state in Canada for over 400 years. Canada has been a constitutional monarchy in its own right since Confederation in 1867 during Queen Victoria's reign. The Crown is a symbol of government, including the legislatures, the courts, Parliament, police services and the Canadian Forces.

Parliament Buildings

The towers, arches, sculptures and stained glass of the Parliament Buildings embody the French, English and Aboriginal traditions and the Gothic Revival architecture popular in the time of Queen Victoria. The buildings were completed in the 1860s. The Centre Block was destroyed by an accidental fire in 1916 and rebuilt in 1922. The Library is the only part of the original building remaining. The Memorial Chamber within the Tower contains the Books of Remembrance in which are written the names of soldiers, sailors and airmen who died serving Canada in wars or while on duty. The Quebec National Assembly is built in the French Second Empire style, while the legislatures of the other provinces are Baroque, Romanesque and neoclassical, reflecting the Greco-Roman heritage of Western civilization in which democracy originated.

Canada's Government System

There are three (3) key facts about Canada's system of government: Canada's country is a federal state, parliamentary democracy, and constitutional monarchy.

The interplay between the three (3) branches of government is the Executive, Legislative, and Judicial. The branches of government, which work together but also, sometimes in creative tension, helps to secure the rights and freedoms of Canadians. Federalism allows different provinces to adopt policies tailored to their own populations, and gives provinces the flexibility to experiment with new ideas and policies.

Majority Government

If the party in power holds at least half of the seats in the House of Commons, this is called a majority government. The Prime Minister and the party in power run the government as long as they have the support or confidence of the majority of the Members of Parliament (MPs). If a majority of the members of the House of Commons vote against a major government decision, the party in power is defeated, which usually results in the Prime Minister asking the Governor General, on behalf of the Sovereign, to call an election.

Minority Government

If the party in power holds less than half of the seats in the House of Commons, this is called a minority government.

Matter of Confidence

When the House of Commons votes on a major issue such as the budget, this is considered a matter of confidence.

The Official Opposition (or Her Majesty's Loyal Opposition)

The opposition party with the most members of the House of Commons is the Official Opposition or Her Majesty's Loyal Opposition. The role of opposition parties is to peacefully oppose or try to improve government proposals. The other parties that are not in power are known as opposition parties.

Governments in Canada

Federal State (Federal/State)

In Canada's federal state, the federal government takes responsibility for matters of national and international concern. These include defence, foreign policy, interprovincial trade and communications, currency, navigation, criminal law and citizenship. In the federal government, the Prime Minister selects the Cabinet ministers and the Prime Minister is responsible for the operations and policy of the government. Cabinet ministers are responsible to the elected representatives, which means they must retain the "confidence of the House" and have to resign if they are defeated in a non-confidence vote.

The Federal Government includes elected officials: Members of Parliament (MPs). Some Responsibilities of the Federal Government include National Defence, Foreign Policy, Citizenship, Policing, Criminal Justice, Aboriginal Affairs, International Trade, Immigration (shared), Agriculture (shared), Environment (shared).

In Canada, the State has traditionally partnered with faith communities to promote social welfare, harmony and mutual respect; provide schools and health care; resettle refugees; and uphold religious freedom, religious expression and freedom of conscience. Canada Health Act ensures common elements and a basic standard of coverage.

Cabinet ministers are responsible for running the federal government departments.
The Prime Minister and Cabinet Ministers are called the Cabinet. They make important decisions about how the country is governed, prepare the budget, propose most new laws,

and their decisions can be questioned by all members of the House of Commons (MPs).

Provincial (Provinces) and Territorial (Territories)

The provinces are responsible for municipal government, education, health, natural resources, property and civil rights, and highways. Every province has its own elected Legislative Assembly, like the House of Commons in Ottawa. Provincial legislatures comprise the Lieutenant Governor, and the elected Assembly. The provincial legislatures are architectural treasures. In each province, the Premier has a role similar to that of the Prime Minister in the federal government.

Lieutenant Governor, appointed by the Governor General on the advice of the Prime Minister, normally for five (5) years, represents the Sovereign in each of the ten (10) provinces. The Lieutenant Governor has a role similar to that of the Governor General.

Territorial (Territories)

The three (3) northern territories, which have small populations, do not have the status of provinces, but their governments and assemblies carry out many of the same functions. In the three (3) territories, the Commissioner represents the federal government and plays a ceremonial role. In Nunavut, in the Northern Territories, the Legislative Assembly chooses a premier and ministers by consensus.

In the three (3) territories, the Commissioner represents the federal government and plays a ceremonial role.

Municipal (Local)

Local or municipal government plays an important role in the lives of Canada's citizens. Municipal governments usually have a council that passes laws called "by-laws" that affect only the local community. The council usually includes a mayor (or a reeve) and councillors or aldermen. Municipalities are normally responsible for urban or regional planning, streets and roads, sanitation (such as garbage removal), snow removal, firefighting, ambulance and other emergency services, recreation facilities, public transit and some local health and social services. Most major urban centres have municipal police forces.

The Municipal (Local) Government includes elected officials: Mayor or Reeve, Councillors or Aldermen. Some Responsibilities of the Municipal (Local) Government include Social and Community Health, Recycling Programs, Transportation and Utilities, Snow Removal, Policing, Firefighting, Emergency Services.

5–5. Man in Feather Headdress.
(Photo by Elena Olesik / Pexels)

Shared Government Responsibilities

Federal and Provincial (Provinces) Governments responsibilities were defined in 1867 in the British North America Act, now known as the Constitution Act, 1867. The federal government and provinces share jurisdiction over agriculture and immigration.

Provincial and Territorial (Territories)

Governments each have an elected legislature where provincial and territorial laws are passed. Publicly funded education is provided by the provinces and territories. Provincial (Provinces) and Territorial (Territories) Governments include elected officials: Members of the Legislative Assembly (MLAs), Members of the National Assembly (MNAs), Members of the Provincial (Ontario, Quebec) Parliament (MPPs), Members of the House of Assembly (MHAs) depending on the province or territory. Some Responsibilities of the Provincial (Provinces) and Territorial (Territories) Governments include Education, Health Care, Natural Resources, Highways, Policing, Property and Civil Rights, Immigration (shared), Agriculture (shared), Environment (shared).

The First Nations

The First Nations have band chiefs and councillors who have major responsibilities on First Nations reserves, including housing, schools and other services. There are a number of provincial, regional and national Aboriginal organizations that are a voice for First Nations, Métis and Inuit people in their relationships with the federal, provincial and territorial governments.

5–6. Assembly of First Nations insignia.
(Photo by Democracy Chronicles. License: Public Domain)

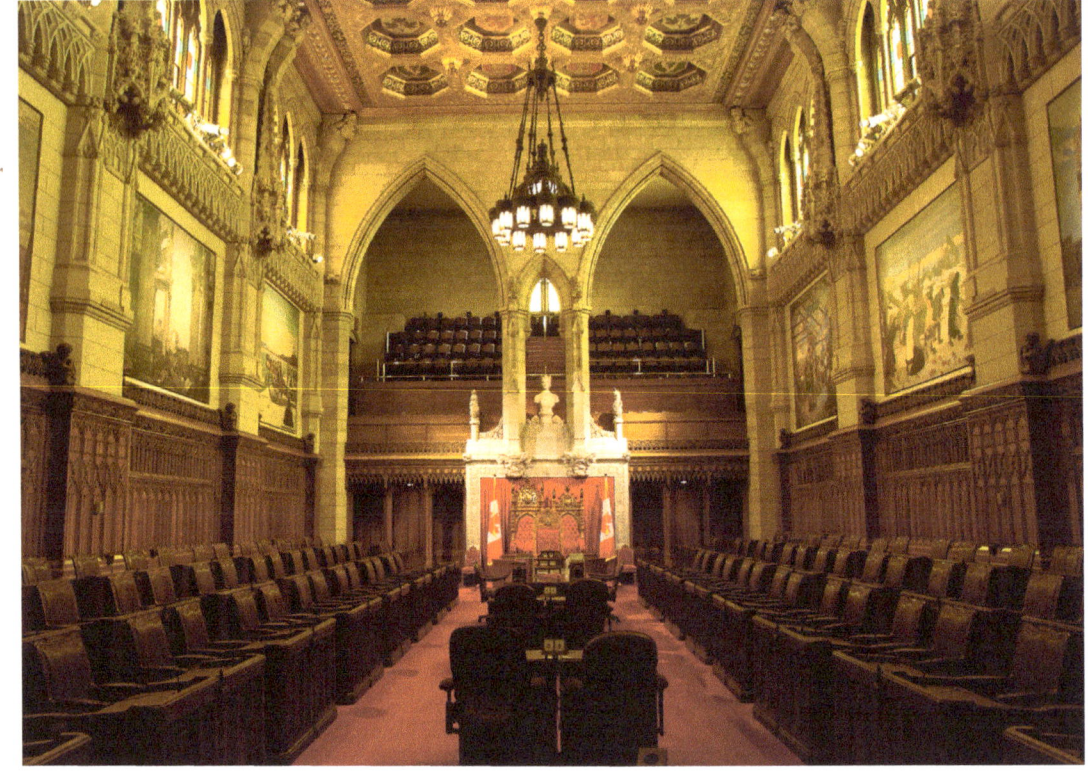

5–7. Senate Chamber.
(Photo by Johnathan Nightingale. © 2009. License: Attribution-ShareAlike 2.0 Generic (CC BY-SA 2.0).
https://www.flickr.com/photos/johnath/3946607810)

Parliamentary Democracy

In Canada's parliamentary democracy, the people elect members to the House of Commons in Ottawa. Also, the people elect members to the provincial and territorial legislatures. These representatives are responsible for passing laws, approving and monitoring expenditures, and keeping the government accountable. Living in a democracy, Canadian citizens have the right and the responsibility to participate in making decisions that affect them. It is important for Canadians, aged 18 or above, to participate in their democracy by voting in federal, provincial or territorial and municipal elections.

Parliament has three (3) parts: the Sovereign (Queen or King), the Senate, and the House of Commons (Members of Parliament, MPs).

5–8. House of Commons, Parliament of Canada.
(Photo by Jonathankslim. © 2012. License: Attribution-ShareAlike 3.0 Unported (CC BY-SA 3.0). https://commons.wikimedia.org/wiki/File:House_of_Common,_Parliament_Canada.jpg)

The Sovereign (Queen or King)

The Sovereign is a part of Parliament, playing an important, non-partisan role as the focus of citizenship and allegiance, most visibly during royal visits to Canada. The Royal Family's example of lifelong service to the community is an encouragement for citizens to give their best to their country.

The Senate

Senators are appointed by the Governor General on the advice of the Prime Minister and serve until age 75.

The House of Commons (Members of Parliament, MPs)

The House of Commons is the representative chamber, made up of members of Parliament elected by the people, traditionally every four years.

Both the Senate and House of Commons consider and review bills (proposals for new laws). No bill can become law in Canada until it has been passed by both chambers and has received royal assent, granted by the Governor General on behalf of the Sovereign.

Constitutional Monarchy

As a constitutional monarchy, Canada's Head of State is a hereditary Sovereign (Queen or King), who reigns in accordance with the Constitution: the rule of law. Her Majesty is a symbol of Canadian sovereignty, a guardian of constitutional freedoms, and a reflection of Canada's history. Canada has been a constitutional monarchy in its own right since Confederation in 1867 during Queen Victoria's reign. As Head of the Commonwealth, the Sovereign links Canada to other nations that cooperate to advance social, economic and cultural progress. Other constitutional monarchies include Denmark, Norway, Sweden, Australia, New Zealand, The Netherlands, Spain, Thailand, Japan, Jordan and Morocco.

Distinction Between the Sovereign and Prime Minister

There is a clear distinction in Canada between the head of state—the Sovereign—and the head of government—the Prime Minister, who actually directs the governing of the country.

The Sovereign: The Queen is the head of state. The Governor General, appointed by the Sovereign on the advice of the Prime Minister, usually for five (5) years, represents the Sovereign in Canada. In each of the ten (10) provinces, the Sovereign is represented by the Lieutenant Governor, who is appointed by the Governor General on the advice of the Prime Minister, also normally for five years.

The Prime Minister: The Prime Minister is the head of government, and actually directs the governing of the country. In the federal government, the Prime Minister selects the Cabinet ministers, chooses the ministers of the Crown with most of them from among members of the House of Commons. In the federal government, the Prime Minister is responsible for the operations and policy of the government, makes important decisions about how the country is governed, prepares the budget, and proposes most new laws.

Major Political Parties

There are three (3) major political parties currently represented in the House of Commons: the Conservative Party, New Democratic Party, and Liberal Party.

The Governor General invites the leader of the political party with the most seats in the House of Commons, ordinarily, after an election, to form the government. After being appointed by the Governor General, the leader of this party becomes the Prime Minister.

Federal Elections

Canadians vote in elections for the people (Members of Parliament, MPs) they want to represent them in the House of Commons. In each election, voters may re-elect the same members of the House of Commons (MPs) or choose new ones. Members of the House of Commons are also known as Members of Parliament or MPs. Under legislation passed by Parliament, federal elections must be held on the third Monday in October every four years following the most recent general election. The Prime Minister may ask the Governor General to call an earlier election. As of this writing, Canada is divided into 338 electoral districts (ridings or constituencies).

On October 27, 2011, the Conservative government proposed Bill C-20, a measure that would expand the House of Commons from 308 to 338 seats, with 15 additional seats for Ontario, 6 additional seats each for Alberta and British Columbia, and 3 for Quebec. The new electoral districts came into effect for the 2015 federal election.

An electoral district is a geographical area represented by a Member of Parliament (MP). The citizens in each electoral district elect one Member of Parliament (MP) who sits in the House of Commons to represent them, as well as all Canadians.

Canadian citizens who are 18 years old or older may run in a federal election. The people who run for office are called candidates. There can be many candidates in an electoral district.

The people in each electoral district vote for the candidate and political party of their choice. The candidate with the most votes becomes the MP for that electoral district.

Voting

At the time of Confederation, the vote was limited to property-owning adult white males — common in most democratic countries at the time. Most Canadians of Asian descent had in the past been denied the vote in federal and provincial elections. The effort by women to achieve the right to vote is known as the women's suffrage movement. Thus, women received the right to vote. Today, every citizen over the age of 18 may vote.

One of the privileges of Canadian citizenship is the right to vote. One is eligible to vote in a federal election or cast a ballot in a federal referendum if one is: a Canadian citizen; at least 18 years old on voting day; and on the voters' list. The voters' lists used during federal elections and referendums are produced from the National Register of Electors by a neutral agency of Parliament called Elections Canada. This is a permanent database of Canadian citizens 18 years of age or older who are qualified to vote in federal elections and referendums.

Once an election has been called, Elections Canada mails a voter information card to each elector whose name is in the National Register of Electors. The card lists when and where you vote and the number to call if you require an interpreter or other special services.

Even if you choose not to be listed in the National Register of Electors or do not receive a voter information card, you can still be added to the voters' list at any time, including on election day.

To vote, either on election day or at advance polls, go to the polling station listed on your voter information card. Bring this card, proof of your identity, and address to the polling station.

Immediately after the polling stations close, election officers count the ballots and the results are announced on radio and television, and in the newspapers.

Ordinarily, after an election the leader of the political party with the most seats in the House of Commons is invited by the Governor General to form the government. After being appointed by the Governor General, the leader of this party becomes the Prime Minister.

Secret Ballot

Canadian law secures the right to a secret ballot. This means that no one can watch you vote, and no one should look at how you voted. One may choose to discuss how they voted with others, but no one, including family members, employer or union representatives, has the right to insist that one tell them how one voted.

Provincial, territorial and municipal elections are held by secret ballot, but the rules are not the same as those for federal elections. It is important to find out the rules for voting in provincial, territorial and local elections so that one can exercise their right to vote.

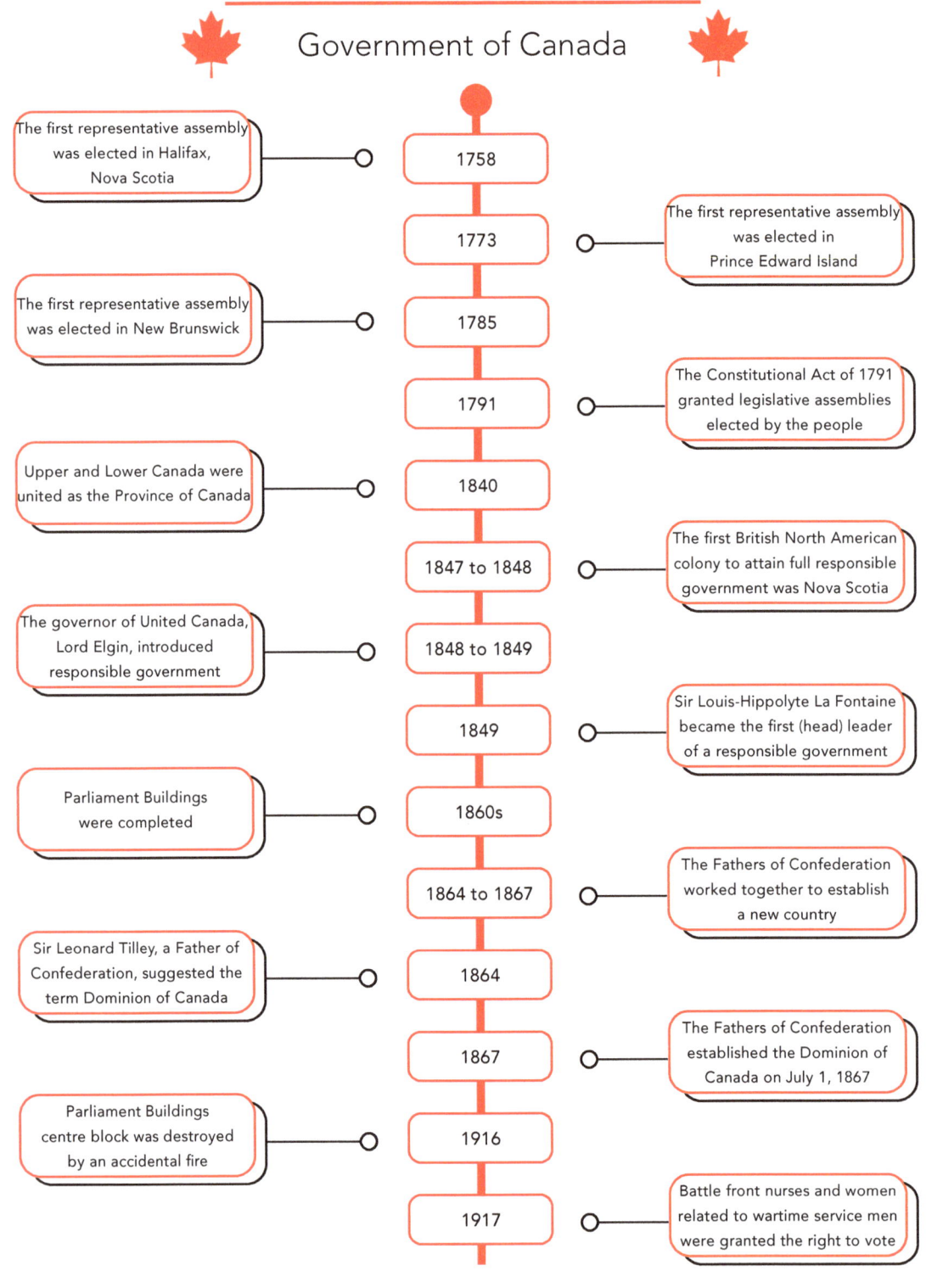

Canada Government

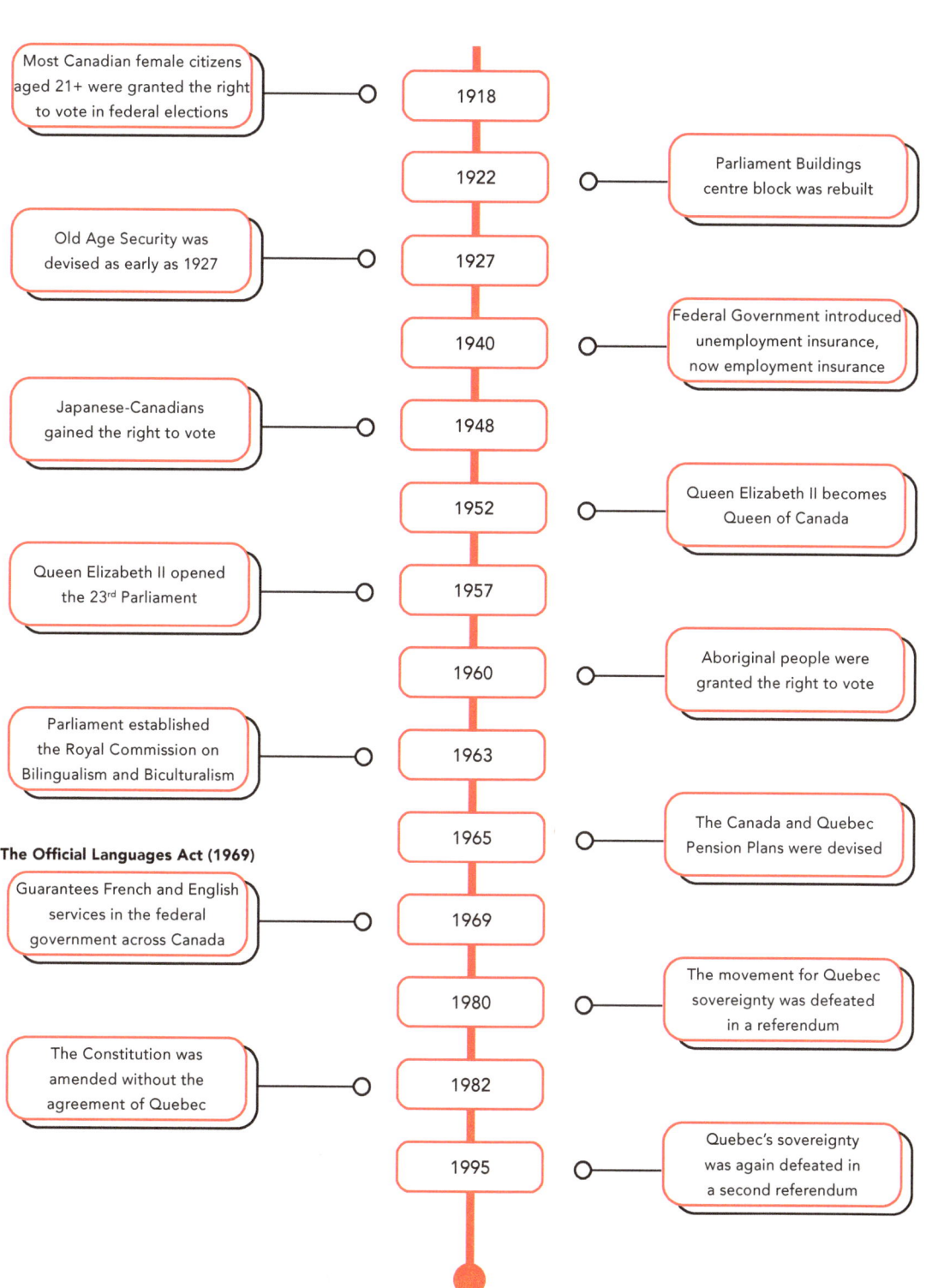

- **1918** — Most Canadian female citizens aged 21+ were granted the right to vote in federal elections
- **1922** — Parliament Buildings centre block was rebuilt
- **1927** — Old Age Security was devised as early as 1927
- **1940** — Federal Government introduced unemployment insurance, now employment insurance
- **1948** — Japanese-Canadians gained the right to vote
- **1952** — Queen Elizabeth II becomes Queen of Canada
- **1957** — Queen Elizabeth II opened the 23rd Parliament
- **1960** — Aboriginal people were granted the right to vote
- **1963** — Parliament established the Royal Commission on Bilingualism and Biculturalism
- **1965** — The Canada and Quebec Pension Plans were devised
- **1969** — **The Official Languages Act (1969)** Guarantees French and English services in the federal government across Canada
- **1980** — The movement for Quebec sovereignty was defeated in a referendum
- **1982** — The Constitution was amended without the agreement of Quebec
- **1995** — Quebec's sovereignty was again defeated in a second referendum

06   Canada Laws

6–1. Canadian criminal cases, 3rd Ed.
(Photo by Raysonho @ Open Grid Scheduler / Grid Engine. License: Public Domain)

Canadian law has several sources: Laws passed by Parliament, the Provincial Legislatures, English Common Law, the Civil Code of France, and the Unwritten Constitution, inherited from Great Britain. The responsibilities of the federal and provincial governments were defined in 1867 in the British North America Act, now known as the Constitution Act, 1867. Habeas Corpus is the right to challenge unlawful detention by the state, and comes from English Common Law. The federal government is required by law to provide services throughout Canada in English and French.

Men and Women are equal under the law. Canada's openness and generosity do not extend to barbaric cultural practises that tolerate spousal, "honour killings," female genital mutilation, forced marriage or other gender-based violence. Those guilty of these crimes are severely punished under Canada's criminal laws.

No person or group is above the law. Individuals and governments are regulated by laws and not by arbitrary actions.

Thus, one of Canada's founding principles is the rule of law — that is, obeying the law.

The Justice System

The Canadian justice system guarantees everyone due process under the law. Canada's judicial system is founded on the presumption of innocence in criminal matters, meaning everyone is innocent until proven guilty.

Canada's legal system is based on a heritage that includes the rule of law, freedom under the law, democratic principles and due process.

Due process is the principle that the government must respect all the legal rights a person is entitled to under the law.

Canada is governed by an organized system of laws. These laws are the written rules intended to guide people in Canada's society. They are made by elected representatives. The law in Canada applies to everyone, including judges, politicians and the police. Canada's laws are intended to provide order in society and a peaceful way to settle disputes, and to express the values and beliefs of Canadians.

Scales of Justice

Lady Justice symbolizes the impartial manner in which Canada's laws are administered: blind to all considerations but the facts.

Courts

The courts settle disputes. The Supreme Court of Canada is Canada's highest court. The Federal Court of Canada deals with matters concerning the federal government. In most provinces there is an appeal court and a trial court, sometimes called the Court of Queen's Bench or the Supreme Court. There are also provincial courts for lesser offences, family courts, traffic courts and small claims courts for civil cases involving small sums of money.

Police

The police are there to keep people safe and to help you. The police are there to enforce the law. You can ask the police for help in all kinds of situations—if there's been an accident, if someone has stolen something from you, if you are a victim of assault, if you see a crime taking place or if someone you know has gone missing.

There are different types of police in Canada, there are provincial police forces in Ontario and Quebec. There are municipal police departments in all provinces. The Royal Canadian Mounted Police (RCMP) enforce federal laws throughout Canada, and serve as the provincial police in all provinces and territories except Ontario and Quebec, as well as in some municipalities.

You can also question the police about their service or conduct if you feel you need to. Almost all police forces in Canada have a process by which you can bring your concerns to the police and seek action.

Making Laws

How a bill becomes law — The Legislative Process

STEP 1 First Reading – The bill is considered read for the first time and is printed.

STEP 2 Second Reading – Members debate the bill's principle.

STEP 3 Committee Stage – Committee members study the bill clause by clause.

STEP 4 Report Stage – Members can make other amendments.

STEP 5 Third Reading – Members debate and vote on the bill.

STEP 6 Senate – The bill follows a similar process in the Senate.

STEP 7 Royal Assent – The bill receives royal assent after being passed by both Houses.

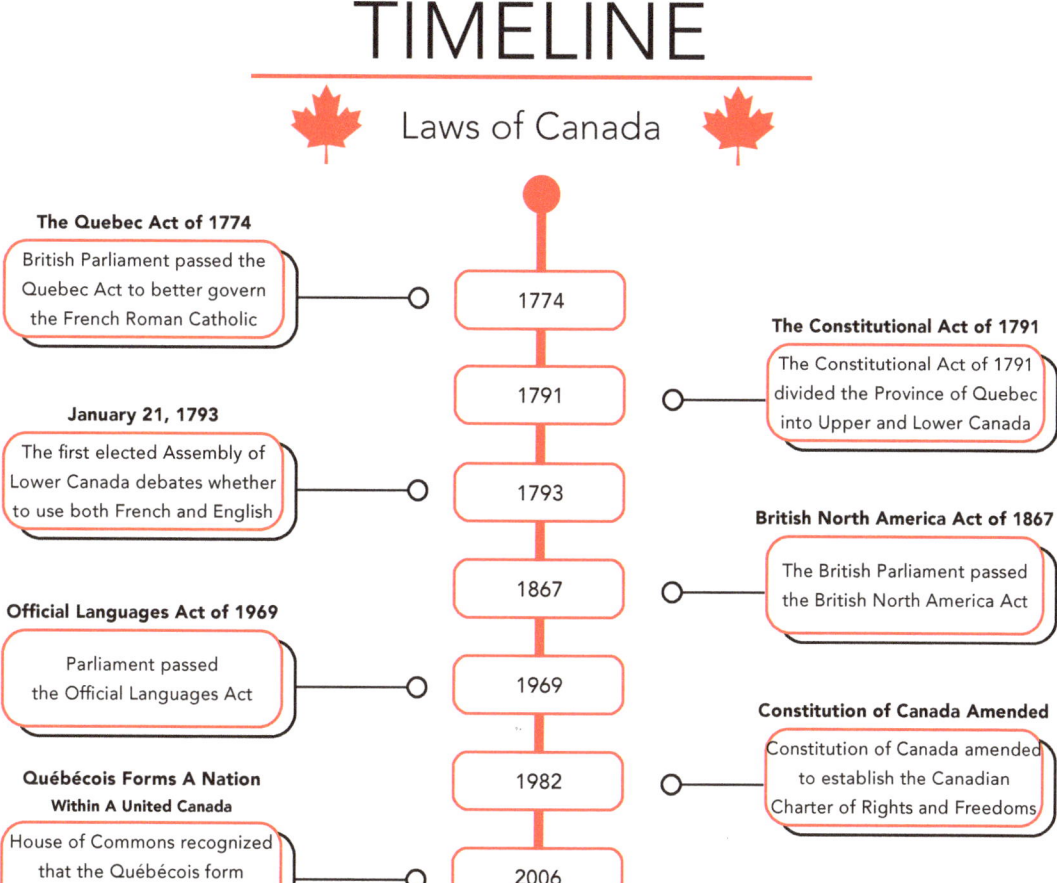

07   Canada Symbols

Canada has many important symbols — objects, events, and people that have special meaning. Together they help explain what it means to be Canadian and express Canada's national identity. Poets and songwriters have hailed Canada as the "Great Dominion."

Symbols

The Beaver

Adopted centuries ago as a symbol of the Hudson's Bay Company, the beaver became an emblem of the St. Jean Baptiste Society, a French-Canadian patriotic association, in 1834, and was also adopted by other groups. This industrious rodent can be seen on the five-cent coin, on the coats of arms of Saskatchewan and Alberta, and of cities such as Montreal and Toronto.

Canada's Official Languages

English and French are the two official languages and important symbols of identity. English speakers (Anglophones) and French speakers (Francophones) have lived together in partnership and creative tension for more than 300 years. Parliament passed the Official Languages Act in 1969 and has three (3) main objectives: Establish equality between French and English in Parliament, the Government of Canada and institutions subject to the Act; Maintain and develop official language minority communities in Canada; and Promote equality of French and English in Canadian society.

The Canadian Crown

The Crown has been a symbol of the state in Canada for over 400 years. Canada has been a constitutional monarchy in its own right since Confederation in 1867 during Queen Victoria's reign. Queen Elizabeth II, has been Queen of Canada since 1952. The Crown is a symbol of government, including Parliament, the legislatures, the courts, police services and the Canadian Forces.

Caribou (Reindeer)

The caribou (reindeer) is popular game for hunters and a symbol of Canada's North.

Coat of Arms and Motto

As an expression of national pride after the First World War, Canada adopted an official coat of arms and a national motto, A mari usque ad mare, which in Latin means "from sea to sea."

7–1. Canadian Pacific Railway 1881 insignia.
[featuring a beaver and maple leaf, two of Canada's national symbols]
(Photo by PxHere. License: Public Domain)

7–2. Flag of Canada.
[featuring the maple leaf]
(Photo by Social Soup Social Media / Pexels)

The arms contain symbols of England, France, Scotland and Ireland as well as red maple leaves. Today the arms can be seen on dollar bills, government documents and public buildings.

Constitutional Monarchy

As a constitutional monarchy, Her Majesty is a symbol of Canadian sovereignty, a guardian of constitutional freedoms, and a reflection of Canada's history. The Royal Family's example of lifelong service to the community is an encouragement for citizens to give their best to their country.

Flags in Canada

The red-white-red pattern of Canada's maple leaf flag, designed by George Stanley, is based on the flag of the Royal Military College in Kingston founded in 1876. Red and white had been colours of France and England since the Middle Ages, and the national colours of Canada since 1921. However, before Confederation, the flag of the Hudson's Bay Company flew over Western Canada for about 200 years. The flag of Canada made its first official appearance on February 15, 1965, and the date is now celebrated annually as National Flag of Canada Day.

The Union Jack is Canada's official Royal Flag and the Canadian Red Ensign served as the Canadian flag for about 100 years. But, a new Canadian flag was raised for the first time in 1965.

The provinces and territories also have flags that embody their distinct traditions.

Canada Symbols

The Fleur-de-Lys

It is said that the lily flower ("fleur-de-lys") was adopted by the French king in the year 496 and became the symbol of French royalty for more than 1,000 years, including the colony of New France. Revived at Confederation, the fleur-de-lys was included in the Canadian Red Ensign. In 1948 Quebec adopted its own flag, based on the Cross and the fleur-de-lys.

The Maple Leaf

The maple leaf is Canada's best-known symbol. Maple leaves were adopted as a symbol by French Canadians in the 1700s. Maple leaves have appeared on Canadian uniforms and insignia since the 1850s. The maple leaves are carved into the headstones of Canada's fallen soldiers buried overseas and in Canada.

National Anthem

O Canada was proclaimed as the national anthem in 1980. It was first sung in Québec City in 1880. French and English Canadians sing different words to the national anthem.

<u>O Canada</u>

O Canada! Our home and native land!
True patriot love in all thy sons command
With glowing hearts we see thee rise
The true North strong and free!
From far and wide, O Canada
We stand on guard for thee
God keep our land glorious and free!
O Canada, we stand on guard for thee
O Canada, we stand on guard for thee

<u>Ô Canada</u>

Ô Canada! Terre de nos aïeux,
Ton front est ceint de fleurons glorieux!
Car ton bras sait porter l'épée,
Il sait porter la croix!
Ton histoire est une épopée
Des plus brillants exploits.
Et ta valeur, de foi trempée,
Protégera nos foyers et nos droits.
Protégera nos foyers et nos droits.

7–3. Fleur-de-lys du Québec, Canada.
(Photo by Gouvernement du Québec and Razorbliss.
License: Public Domain)

7–4. O Canada.
(Photo by Calixa Lavallée. Toronto: G. V. Thompson.
Library and Archives Canada, csm4577.3. © 2008.
License: Attribution 2.0 Generic (CC BY 2.0).
https://www.flickr.com/photos/lac-bac/14411402284)

Important Dates

Sir John A. Macdonald Day – January 11

Vimy Day – April 9

Victoria Day – Monday preceding May 25
(Sovereign's birthday)

Fête nationale (Quebec) – June 24
(Feast of St. John the Baptist)

Canada Day – July 1

Thanksgiving Day – Second Monday of October

Remembrance Day – November 11

Sir Wilfrid Laurier Day – November 20

Boxing Day – December 26

The Orders of Canada and Other Honours

Official awards are called honours, consisting of orders, decorations and medals. After using British honours for many years, Canada started its own honours system with the Order of Canada in 1967, the centennial of Confederation.

Parliament Buildings

The towers, arches, sculptures and stained glass of the Parliament Buildings embody the French, English, and Aboriginal traditions and the Gothic Revival architecture popular in the time of Queen Victoria. The buildings were completed in the 1860s. The Centre Block was destroyed by an accidental fire in 1916 and rebuilt in 1922. The Library is the only part of the original building remaining. The Peace Tower was completed in 1927 in memory of the First World War. The Memorial Chamber within the Tower contains the Books of Remembrance in which are written the names of soldiers, sailors and airmen who died serving Canada in wars or while on duty.

7–5. A coin of the Seal of the Order of Canada.
(Photo by Ctjj.stevenson. © 2019. License: Attribution-ShareAlike 4.0 International (CC BY-SA 4.0). https://en.wikipedia.org/wiki/File:A_coin_of_the_Seal_of_the_Order_of_Canada.png)

7–6. Peace Arch Park. Taken on the U.S. side (Blaine, WA).
(Photo by David Herrera. © 2008.
License: Attribution 2.0 Generic (CC BY 2.0).
https://www.flickr.com/photos/dph1110/2672773090)

7–7. Peace Arch - USA and Canada border. [Taken on the Canada side]
(Photo by Iain Cameron. © 2018.
License: Attribution 2.0 Generic (CC BY 2.0).
https://www.flickr.com/photos/igcameron/29979119118)

The provincial legislatures are architectural treasures. The Quebec National Assembly is built in the French Second Empire style, while the legislatures of the other provinces are Baroque, Romanesque and neoclassical, reflecting the Greco-Roman heritage of Western civilization in which democracy originated.

Peace Arch

Peace Arch, at Blaine in the State of Washington, is inscribed with the words "children of a common mother" and "brethren dwelling together in unity," symbolizes Canada's close ties and common interests.

Popular Sports

Hockey is Canada's most popular spectator sport and considered the national winter sport. Ice hockey was developed in Canada in the 1800s. The National Hockey League played for the championship Stanley Cup, donated by Lord Stanley, the Governor General, in 1892. The Clarkson Cup, established in 2005 by Adrienne Clarkson, the 26th Governor General (and the first of Asian origin), was awarded for women's hockey.

Canadian football is the second most popular sport. Curling, an ice game introduced by Scottish pioneers, is popular. Lacrosse, an ancient sport first played by Aboriginals, is the official summer sport. And, soccer has the most registered players of any game in Canada.

Remembrance Day

Remembrance Day is each year on November 11. Canadians remember the sacrifices of Canada's veterans and brave fallen in all wars up to the present day in which Canadians took part, wear the red poppy, and observe a moment of silence at the 11th hour of the 11th day of the 11th month to honour the sacrifices of over a million brave men and women who have served, and the approximate 110,000 who have given their lives. Canadian medical officer Lieutenant-Colonel John McCrae composed the poem "In Flanders Fields" in 1915—it is often recited on Remembrance Day:

In Flanders fields the poppies blow
Between the crosses, row on row,
That mark our place; and in the sky
The larks, still bravely singing, fly
Scarce heard amid the guns below.
We are the dead. Short days ago
We lived, felt dawn, saw sunset glow,
Loved, and were loved, and now we lie
In Flanders fields.
Take up our quarrel with the foe:
To you from failing hands we throw
The torch; be yours to hold it high.
If ye break faith with us who die
We shall not sleep, though poppies grow
In Flanders fields.

Royal Anthem

The Royal Anthem of Canada, "God Save the Queen (or King)," can be played or sung on any occasion when Canadians wish to honour the Sovereign.

God Save the Queen

God save our gracious Queen!
Long live our noble Queen!
God save the Queen!
Send her victorious,
Happy and glorious,
Long to reign over us,
God save the Queen!

Dieu protège la Reine

Dieu protège la Reine!
De sa main souveraine!
Vive la Reine!
Qu'un règne glorieux,
Long et victorieux,
Rende son peuple heureux,
Vive la Reine!

The Royal Canadian Mounted Police (RCMP or "the Mounties")

The Royal Canadian Mounted Police are the national police force and one of Canada's best-known symbols.

Scales of Justice

The blindfolded Lady Justice symbolizes the impartial manner in which Canada's laws are administered: blind to all considerations but the facts.

The Victoria Cross

The Victoria Cross (V.C.) is the highest honour available to Canadians and is awarded for the most conspicuous bravery, a daring or pre-eminent act of valour or self-sacrifice, or extreme devotion to duty in the presence of the enemy. As of this writing, the V.C. has been awarded to 99 Canadians, since instituted in 1856 by Queen Victoria, including:

7–8. Lt. Alexander Dunn V.C., 11th Hussars 1854.
(Photo by Unknown Author. License: Public Domain)

7–9. William Hall V.C.
[Between 1857 and 1904]
(Photo by Unknown Photographer. License: Public Domain)

Lieutenant (Colonel) Alexander Roberts Dunn, V.C., born in present-day Toronto, served in the British Army in the Charge of the Light Brigade at Balaclava (1854) in the Crimean War, and was the first Canadian to be awarded the Victoria Cross.

Able Seaman William Hall, of Horton, Nova Scotia, whose parents were American slaves, was the first black man to be awarded the V.C. for his role in the Siege of Lucknow during the Indian Rebellion of 1857.

Corporal Filip Konowal, promoted Sergeant, was born in Ukraine, showed exceptional courage in the Battle of Hill 70 in 1917, and became the first member of the Canadian Corps not born in the British Empire to be awarded the V.C.

Air Marshal William A. Bishop, better known as Flying Ace Captain Billy Bishop, V.C., was born in Owen Sound, Ontario, earned the V.C. in the Royal Flying Corps during the First World War, and was later an honorary Air Marshal of the Royal Canadian Air Force.

7-10. Filip Konowal V.C.
(Photo by Elliot & Fry. License: Public Domain)

7-11. Air Marshal William Avery Bishop V.C.
(Photo by Alphonse Jongers. License: Public Domain)

7-12. Major Paul Triquet V.C. 1944.
(Photo by Unknown Author. License: Public Domain)

7-13. Robert Hampton Gray V.C.
[Before his death in 1945]
(Photo by Canadian Government. License: Public Domain)

Captain Paul Triquet, of Cabano, Quebec, earned the V.C. leading his men and a handful of tanks in the attack on Casa Berardi, Italy in 1943 during the Second World War. He later became a Brigadier.

Lieutenant Robert Hampton Gray, a navy pilot, born in Trail, B.C., was killed while bombing and sinking a Japanese warship in August 1945, a few days before the end of the Second World War. He is the last Canadian to receive the V.C. to date.

In 1993, Canada adopted its own national version of the Victoria Cross. The Canadian V.C. has not yet been awarded.

08   Canada Arts and Culture

8–1. Kenojuak Ashevak: Window at John Bell Chapel of Appleby College in Oakville (Ontario) near Toronto (Canada).
(Photo by Ansgar Walk. © 2004, 2008.
License: Attribution-ShareAlike 3.0 Unported (CC BY-SA 3.0).
https://commons.wikimedia.org/wiki/
File:Kenojuak_Fenster_%28Oakville%29.jpg)

Arts

In the visual arts, Canada is historically perhaps best known for the Group of Seven, founded in 1920, who developed a style of painting to capture the rugged wilderness landscapes. Emily Carr painted the forests and Aboriginal artifacts of the West Coast.

Les Automatistes of Quebec were pioneers of modern abstract art in the 1950s, most notably Jean-Paul Riopelle.

Men and women of letters included Stephen Leacock, Louis Hémon, Sir Charles G.D. Roberts, Pauline Johnson, Émile Nelligan, Robertson Davies, Margaret Laurence and Mordecai Richler.

Musicians such as Sir Ernest MacMillan and Healey Willan won renown in Canada and abroad.

Writers such as Joy Kogawa, Michael Ondaatje and Rohinton Mistry have diversified Canada's literary experience.

Louis-Philippe Hébert was celebrated as a sculptor of historical figures.

Kenojuak Ashevak pioneered modern Inuit art with etchings, prints and soapstone sculptures.

Denys Arcand films, popular in Quebec and across the country, have won international awards. Other noteworthy Canadian filmmakers include Norman Jewison and Atom Egoyan.

8–2. Dr. James Naismith, inventor of basketball (sculpture).
Sculptor: Elden Tefft; Lawrence, Kansas; dedicated July 23, 2011.
(Photo by D. Gordon E. Robertson. © 2012. License: Attribution-ShareAlike 3.0 Unported (CC BY-SA 3.0).
https://en.wikipedia.org/wiki/File:Naismith_statue,_Almonte.jpg)

Sports

Basketball was invented by Canadian James Naismith in 1891. And, professional teams in the Canadian Football League (CFL) competed for the championship Grey Cup, donated by Lord Grey, the Governor General, in 1909.

Paul Henderson, in 1972, scored the winning goal for Canada in the Canada-Soviet Summit Series. This goal is often referred to as "the goal heard around the world" and is still remembered today as an important event in both sports and cultural history.

Wayne Gretzky, one of the greatest hockey players of all time, played for the Edmonton Oilers from 1979 to 1988.

In 1980, Terry Fox, a British Columbian who lost his right leg to cancer at the age of 18, began a cross-country run, the "Marathon of Hope," to raise money for cancer research. He became a hero to Canadians. While he did not finish the run and ultimately lost his battle with cancer, his legacy continues through yearly fundraising events in his name.

In 1985, fellow British Columbian Rick Hansen circled the globe in a wheelchair to raise funds for spinal cord research.

In 1996 at the Olympic Summer Games, Donovan Bailey became a world record sprinter and double Olympic gold medallist.

Catriona Le May Doan carried the flag after winning a gold medal in speed skating at the 2002 Olympic Winter Games.

Chantal Petitclerc became a world champion wheelchair racer and Paralympic gold medalist.

Mark Tewksbury is an Olympic gold medallist, and a prominent activist for gay and lesbian Canadians.

Great Canadian Thinkers and Scientists

Marshall McLuhan and Harold Innis were pioneer thinkers.

Gerhard Herzberg, a refugee from Nazi Germany, John Polanyi, Sidney Altman, Richard E. Taylor, Michael Smith and Bertram Brockhouse were Nobel Prize-winning scientists.

Great Canadian Discoveries and Inventions

Alexander Graham Bell hit on the idea of the telephone at his summer house in Canada.

Dr. John A. Hopps invented the first cardiac pacemaker, used today to save the lives of people with heart disorders.

Dr. Wilder Penfield was a pioneering brain surgeon at McGill University in Montreal, and was known as "the greatest living Canadian."

Joseph-Armand Bombardier invented the snowmobile, a light-weight winter vehicle.

Matthew Evans and Henry Woodward, together, invented the first electric light bulb and later sold the patent to Thomas Edison who, more famously, commercialized the light bulb.

Mike Lazaridis and Jim Balsillie of Research in Motion (RIM), a wireless communications company, is best known for its most famous invention the BlackBerry.

Reginald Fessenden contributed to the invention of radio, sending the first wireless voice message in the world.

8–3. Bell on the telephone in New York (calling Chicago) in 1892.
(Photo by Gilbert H. Grosvenor Collection, Prints and Photographs Division, Library of Congress. License: Public Domain)

8–4. Photograph of C.H. Best and F.G. Banting ca. 1924.
(Photo by Thomas Fisher Rare Book Library. © 1924, 1925, 2014. License: Attribution 2.0 Generic (CC BY 2.0).
https://commons.wikimedia.org/wiki/File:Photograph_of_C.H._Best_and_F.G._Banting_ca._1924_(12309018974).jpg)

Sir Sandford Fleming invented the worldwide system of standard time zones.

Sir Frederick Banting of Toronto and Charles Best discovered insulin, a hormone to treat diabetes that has saved over 16 million lives worldwide.

SPAR Aerospace / National Research Council invented the Canadarm, a robotic arm used in outer space. Since 1989, the Canadian Space Agency and Canadian astronauts have participated in space exploration often using the Canadian-designed and built Canadarm.

The prosperity and diversity of Canada depend on all Canadians working together to face challenges of the future. In seeking to become a citizen, you are joining a country that, with your active participation, will continue to grow and thrive.

09   Canada Facts

9–1. Woman Draped In A Flag Of Canada.
(Photo by Andre Furtado / Canva)

Canada is a constitutional monarchy, parliamentary democracy, and a federal state. Canada has inherited the oldest continuous constitutional tradition in the world. Canada is the only constitutional monarchy in North America with Democratic Institutions including Parliament, Provincial Legislatures, Federal, Territorial, and Local systems of government. Canadians are bound together by a shared commitment to the rule of law and to the institutions of parliamentary government. Institutions uphold a commitment to Peace, Order and Good Government, a key phrase in Canada's original constitutional document in 1867, the British North America Act. Canadians must obey Canada's laws and respect the rights and freedoms of others. Canada is known around the world as a strong and free country.

Canada's three (3) founding peoples are Aboriginal, French, and British. Thus, English and French define the reality of day-to-day life for most people and the country's official languages. Anglophones (English speakers) are generally referred to as "English Canadians," while Francophones (French speakers) are generally referred to as "French Canadiens."

Since the 1800s, the majority of Canadians were born in Canada, but some Canadians immigrate from places where they have experienced warfare or conflict. The first movement to abolish the transatlantic slave trade emerged in the British Parliament in the late 1700s, as thousands of slaves escaped from the United States, following "the North Star" and settling

9–2. Maple Leaf fall.
(Photo by Lewis Parsons / Unsplash)

in Canada via the Underground Railroad, a Christian anti-slavery network. The Canadian Pacific Railway (CPR) project was financed by British and American investors and built by both European and Chinese labour. Afterwards the Chinese were subject to discrimination, including the Head Tax, a race-based entry fee. The Government of Canada apologized in 2006 for this discriminatory policy. After many years of heroic work, the Canadian Pacific Railway's (CPR's) "ribbons of steel" fulfilled a national dream. The railway made it possible for immigrants, including Ukrainians, Poles and thousands from Germany, France, Norway and Sweden, to settle in the West before 1914 and develop a thriving agricultural sector. And, with the Communist victory in the Vietnam War in 1975 many Vietnamese fled seeking refuge in Canada. Thus, such experiences do not justify bringing to Canada violent, extreme or hateful prejudices. Therefore, newcomers are expected to embrace democratic principles such as the rule of law.

A belief in ordered liberty, enterprise, hard work and fair play has enabled Canadians to build a prosperous society in a rugged environment from Canada's Atlantic shores to the Pacific Ocean and to the Arctic Circle. Canadians take pride in their unique identity and have made sacrifices to defend their way of life. Poets and songwriters have hailed Canada as the "Great Dominion."

Heads of State of Canada

The reigning British monarch is Canada's legal head of state. The governor general is the acting, or de facto, head of state.

Monarchs

The monarch is a member of the House of Windsor, a family believed to have been chosen by God to rule the United Kingdom and various other countries. When the current monarch dies or resigns, the oldest son or daughter of the monarch usually takes over – details are spelled out in the Act of Settlement.

MONARCH	REIGN	LENGTH	BORN/DIED
Queen Victoria	June 20, 1837 – Jan. 22, 1901	63 years	1819 – 1901
King Edward VII	Jan. 22, 1901 – May 6, 1910	9 years	1841 – 1910
King George V	May 6, 1910 – Jan. 20, 1936	25 years	1865 – 1936
King Edward VIII	Jan. 20, 1936 – Dec. 11, 1936	10 months	1894 – 1972
King George VI	Dec. 11, 1936 – Feb. 6, 1952	15 years	1895 – 1952
Queen Elizabeth II	Feb. 6, 1952 –	70+ years	1926 –

Governors General of Canada (Canadian, 1952 –)

Men and women who have held the office of Governor General of Canada since it began being filled by Canadian citizens appointed by the Prime Minister of Canada.

NAME	SERVED	BORN/DIED	APPOINTED BY
Vincent Massey	Feb. 28, 1952 – Sept. 15, 1959	1887 – 1967	Louis St. Laurent
Georges Vanier	Sept. 15, 1959 – March 5, 1967	1888 – 1967	John Diefenbaker
Robert Taschereau (acting)	March 5, 1967 – April 17, 1967	1896 – 1970	(automatic succession)
Roland Michener	April 17, 1967 – Jan. 14, 1974	1900 – 1991	Lester Pearson
Jules Legar	Jan. 14, 1974 – Jan. 21, 1979	1913 – 1980	Pierre Trudeau
Edward Schreyer	Jan. 21, 1979 – May 14, 1984	1935 –	Pierre Trudeau
Jeanne Sauve	May 14, 1984 – Jan. 29, 1990	1922 – 1993	Pierre Trudeau
Ray Hynatschen	Jan. 29, 1990 – Feb. 8, 1995	1934 – 2002	Brian Mulroney
Romeo LeBlanc	Feb. 8, 1995 – Oct. 7, 1999	1927 – 2009	Jean Chrétien
Adrienne Clarkson	Oct. 7, 1999 – Sept. 27, 2005	1939 –	Jean Chrétien
Michaëlle Jean	Sept. 27, 2005 – Oct. 1, 2010	1957 –	Paul Martin
David Johnston	Oct. 1, 2010 – Oct. 2, 2017	1941 –	Stephen Harper
Julie Payette	Oct. 2, 2017 – Jan. 21, 2021	1963 –	Justin Trudeau
Richard Wagner (acting)	Jan. 21, 2021 – July 26, 2021	1957 –	(automatic succession)
Mary May Simon	July 26, 2021 –	1947 –	Justin Trudeau

Governors General of Canada (Canadian, 1952 –)

Prime Ministers of Canada

NAME	TENURE	PARTY	BORN/DIED
John A. Macdonald	July 1, 1867 – Nov. 7, 1873	Conservative	1815 – 1891
Alexander Mackenzie	Nov. 7, 1873 – Oct. 10, 1878	Liberal	1822 – 1892
Macdonald (2nd time)	Oct. 17, 1878 – June 6, 1891	Conservative	
John Abbott	June 16, 1891 – Dec. 5, 1892	Conservative	1821 – 1893
John Thompson	Dec. 5, 1892 – Dec. 12, 1894	Conservative	1844 – 1894
Mackenzie Bowell	Dec. 21, 1894 – May 1, 1896	Conservative	1823 – 1917
Charles Tupper	May 1, 1896 – July 11, 1896	Conservative	1821 – 1915
Wilfrid Laurier	July 11, 1896 – Oct. 10, 1911	Liberal	1841 – 1919
Robert Borden	Oct. 10, 1911 – July 10, 1020	Conservative	1854 – 1937
Arthur Meighen	July 10, 1920 – Dec. 29, 1921	Conservative	1874 – 1960
Mackenzie King	Dec. 29, 1921 – June 28, 1926	Liberal	1874 – 1950
Meighen (2nd time)	June 28, 1926 – Sept. 25, 1926	Conservative	
King (2nd time)	Sept. 25, 1926 – Aug. 7, 1930	Liberal	
R.B. Bennett	Aug. 7, 1930 – Oct. 23, 1935	Conservative	1870 – 1947
King (3rd time)	Oct. 23, 1935 – Nov. 15, 1948	Liberal	
Louis St. Laurent	Nov. 15, 1948 – June 21, 1957	Liberal	1882 – 1973
John G. Diefenbaker	June 21, 1957 – April 22, 1963	Progressive Conservative	1895 – 1979
Lester B. Pearson	April 22, 1963 – April 20, 1968	Liberal	1897 – 1972
Pierre Elliott Trudeau	April 20, 1968 – June 4, 1979	Liberal	1919 – 2000
Joe Clark	June 4, 1979 – March 3, 1980	Progressive Conservative	1939 –
Trudeau (2nd time)	March 3, 1980 – June 30, 1984	Liberal	
John Turner	June 30, 1984 – Sept. 17, 1984	Liberal	1929 – 2020
Brian Mulroney	Sept. 17, 1984 – June 25, 1993	Progressive Conservative	1939 –
Kim Campbell	June 25, 1993 – Nov. 4, 1993	Progressive Conservative	1947 –
Jean Chrétien	Nov. 4, 1993 – Dec. 12, 2003	Liberal	1934 –
Paul Martin	Dec. 12, 2003 – Feb. 6, 2006	Liberal	1938 –
Stephen Harper	Feb. 6, 2006 – Nov. 4, 2015	Conservative Party of Canada	1959 –
Justin Trudeau	Nov. 4, 2015 –	Liberal	1971 –

Study Questions and Answers

Section 15 of the Citizenship Regulations

Knowledge of Canada and citizenship criteria

15. (1) A person is considered to have an adequate knowledge of Canada if they demonstrate, based on their responses to questions prepared by the Minister, that they know the national symbols of Canada and have a general understanding of the following subjects: (a) the chief characteristics of Canadian political and military history; (b) the chief characteristics of Canadian social and cultural history; (c) the chief characteristics of Canadian physical and political geography; (d) the chief characteristics of the Canadian system of government as a constitutional monarchy; and (e) characteristics of Canada other than those referred to in paragraphs (a) to (d).

(2) A person is considered to have an adequate knowledge of the responsibilities and privileges of citizenship if they demonstrate, based on their responses to questions prepared by the Minister, that they have a general understanding of the following subjects: (a) participation in the Canadian democratic process; (b) participation in Canadian society, including volunteerism, respect for the environment and the protection of Canada's natural, cultural and architectural heritage; (c) respect for the rights, freedoms and obligations set out in the laws of Canada; and (d) the responsibilities and privileges of citizenship other than those referred to in paragraphs (a) to (c).

1. What are three (3) responsibilities of citizenship? Obeying the law, taking responsibility for oneself and one's family, serving on a jury. *[pp. 2–3]*

2. What is the meaning of the Remembrance Day poppy? To remember the sacrifice of Canadians who have served or died in wars up to the present day. *[p. 88]*

3. How are Members of Parliament chosen? They are elected by voters in their local constituency (riding). *[p. 74]*

4. Name two (2) key documents that contain Canada's rights and freedoms. The Canadian Charter of Rights and Freedoms and Great Charter of Freedoms. *[pp. 2, 5]*

5. Identify four (4) rights that Canadians enjoy. Mobility Rights, Official Language Rights, Minority Language Educational Rights, and Legal Rights. *[pp. 5, 79]*

As a bonus, Right to Vote. *[p. 74]*

6. Name four (4) fundamental freedoms that Canadians enjoy. Freedom of conscience and religion; Freedom of thought, belief, opinion and expression, including freedom of speech and of the press; Freedom of peaceful assembly; and Freedom of association. *[p. 2]*

7. What is meant by the equality of women and men? Women and men are equal under the law. *[p. 5]*

8. What are some examples of taking responsibility for yourself and your family? Getting a job. Taking care of one's family. Working hard in keeping with one's abilities. *[p. 2]*

9. Who were the founding peoples of Canada? Aboriginal, French, and British. *[p. 16]*

10. Who are the Métis? A distinct people of mixed Aboriginal and European ancestry. The Métis come from both French-and English-speaking backgrounds. *[p. 23]*

11. What does the word "Inuit" mean? "The people" in the Inuktitut language. *[p. 16]*

12. What is meant by the term "responsible government"? The ministers of the Crown must have the support of a majority of the elected representatives in order to govern [Lord Durham]. If the government loses a confidence vote in the assembly it must resign [Lord Elgin]. *[p. 62]*

13. Who was Sir Louis-Hippolyte La Fontaine? The first (head) leader of a responsible government (similar to a prime minister) in Canada in 1849. He was a reformer, and worked with British governors toward responsible government. Also, he was a champion of democracy and French language rights. *[p. 28]*

Study Questions and Answers (continued)

14. What did the Canadian Pacific Railway symbolize? Unity. On November 7, 1885, a powerful symbol of unity was completed when Donald Smith (Lord Strathcona), the director of the Canadian Pacific Railway (CPR), drove the last spike. *[p. 15]*

15. What does Confederation mean? New Country - the Dominion of Canada. The old Province of Canada was split into two new provinces: Ontario and Quebec, and together with New Brunswick and Nova Scotia formed the new country called the Dominion of Canada. *[pp. 62–63]*

16. What is the significance of the discovery of insulin by Sir Frederick Banting and Charles Best? Insulin is a hormone to treat diabetes, that has saved lives worldwide. Sir Frederick Banting of Toronto and Charles Best discovered insulin, a hormone to treat diabetes that has saved over 16 million lives worldwide. *[p. 98]*

17. What does it mean to say that Canada is a constitutional monarchy? As a constitutional monarchy, Her Majesty is a symbol of Canadian sovereignty, a guardian of constitutional freedoms, and a reflection of Canada's history. *[p. 73]*

18. What are the three (3) branches of government? Executive, Legislative, and Judicial. *[p. 65]*

19. What is the difference between the role of the Queen and that of the Prime Minister? The Sovereign is the head of state, represented in Canada by the Governor General, who is appointed by the Sovereign on the advice of the Prime Minister, usually for five years. In each of the ten provinces, the Sovereign is represented by the Lieutenant Governor, who is appointed by the Governor General on the advice of the Prime Minister, also normally for five years.

The Prime Minister is the head of government, and actually directs the governing of the country. In the federal government, the Prime Minister selects the Cabinet ministers, chooses the ministers of the Crown, most of them from among members of the House of Commons, and is responsible for the operations and policy of the government. That is, the Prime Minister makes important decisions about how the country is governed, prepares the budget, and proposes most new laws. *[p. 73]*

20. What is the highest honour that Canadians can receive? The Victoria Cross. The Victoria Cross (V.C.) is the highest honour available to Canadians and is awarded for the most conspicuous bravery, a daring or pre-eminent act of valour or self-sacrifice, or extreme devotion to duty in the presence of the enemy. *[p. 89]*

Study Questions and Answers

21. When you go to vote on election day, what do you do? Go to your polling station (the location on your voter information card). Bring your voter information card and proof of your identity and address to the polling station. *[p. 75]*

22. Who is entitled to vote in Canadian federal elections? A Canadian citizen, at least 18 years old on voting day, and on the voters' list. *[p. 74]*

23. In Canada, are you obliged to tell other people how you voted? No. You may choose to discuss how you voted with others, but no one, including family members, your employer or union representative, has the right to insist that you tell them how you voted. *[p. 75]*

24. After an election, which party forms the government? After an election, the leader of the political party with the most seats in the House of Commons is invited by the Governor General to form the government. *[p. 75]*

25. What are the three (3) levels of government? Federal, Provincial (Provinces) and Territorial (Territories), and Municipal (Local). *[p. 66–67]*

26. What is the role of the courts in Canada? The courts settle disputes. *[p. 79]*

27. In Canada, are you allowed to question the police about their service or conduct? Yes. You can question the police about their service or conduct if you feel you need to. *[p. 79]*

28. Name two (2) Canadian symbols. The Canadian Crown (The Crown) is a symbol of government, including Parliament, the legislatures, the courts, police services and the Canadian Forces. The Maple Leaf is Canada's best-known symbol. Maple leaves were adopted as a symbol by French Canadians in the 1700s, have appeared on Canadian uniforms and insignia since the 1850s, and are carved into the headstones of our fallen soldiers buried overseas and in Canada. *[p. 82–89]*

As a bonus, the Royal Canadian Mounted Police (RCMP or "the Mounties") are the national police force and one of Canada's best-known symbols. *[p. 89]*

29. What provinces are referred to as the Atlantic Provinces? Newfoundland and Labrador, Prince Edward Island, Nova Scotia, and New Brunswick. *[pp. 43, 45]*

Epilogue

After the citizenship ceremony, you should find information and services for new citizens such as applying for a passport and voting in an election.

Before you can apply for a passport, you must wait to receive your citizenship certificate after the citizenship ceremony. A valid Canadian passport proves you have the right to enter Canada. However, your citizenship certificate is not a travel document. If you are a dual Canadian citizen, you can only enter Canada with a valid Canadian passport, or special authorization (issued only under certain circumstances).

Registering to vote, as a Canadian citizen, gives you the right and responsibility to vote. For provincial or territorial elections contact the election authority in your province or territory.

As newcomers of Canada, Canadian citizens have an obligation to contribute to Canada. So, now that you are a citizen, think about how will you make your contribution to the country. Also, think about becoming active in your community, that is getting involved with your community to make Canada a stronger and more inclusive country.

But, don't forget to enjoy the wonders of natural and cultural heritage places in Canada. Experience Canadian culture and celebrate your Canadian citizenship. Go to museums, science centres, art galleries and parks across Canada. Valid for new citizens, download Canoo (https://canoo.ca/). Canoo is an app that provides newcomers to Canada with free VIP access to Canada's most exciting cultural and outdoor experiences. Canoo is offered to new Canadian Citizens in the first 12 months of citizenship. Be sure to find out about other services and information for Canadians.

Epilogue

Bibliography

Research

After the citizenship ceremony; https://www.canada.ca/en/immigration-refugees-citizenship/services/canadian-citizenship/become-canadian-citizen/after-citizenship-ceremony.html; June 2022. Find out about information and services for new Canadians.

Apply for Canadian citizenship; https://www.canada.ca/en/immigration-refugees-citizenship/services/canadian-citizenship/become-canadian-citizen.html; June 2022. Who can apply, how to apply, forms, fees and processing times.

Canadian Recipients of the Victoria Cross; https://www.thecanadianencyclopedia.ca/en/article/victoria-cross; July 2022. In total, there have been 99 Canadian recipients of the Victoria Cross. In 1993, Canada adopted its own national version of the Victoria Cross. The Canadian V.C. has not yet been awarded.

Current Constituencies; https://www.ourcommons.ca/members/en/constituencies; July 2022. Canada is divided into 338 electoral districts, also known as constituencies or ridings, and each is entitled to one seat in the House of Commons. Members of Parliament are elected to represent Canadians living in each constituency.

Heads of State of Canada: Monarchs and Governors General of Canada (Canadian, 1952 –); https://thecanadaguide.com/data/heads-of-state; May 2022. The reigning British monarch is Canada's legal head of state. The governor general is the acting, or de facto, head of state. Men and women who have held the office of Governor General of Canada since it began being filled by Canadian citizens appointed by the Prime Minister of Canada.

Official Website of the Government of Canada; Canadian Citizenship; https://www.canada.ca/en/immigration-refugees-citizenship/services/canadian-citizenship.html; June 2022. Apply to become a Canadian citizen.

Prepare for the citizenship ceremony; https://www.canada.ca/en/immigration-refugees-citizenship/services/canadian-citizenship/become-canadian-citizen/citizenship-ceremony.html; June 2022. Who must attend, what happens at the ceremony.

Prepare for the citizenship test and interview; https://www.canada.ca/en/immigration-refugees-citizenship/services/canadian-citizenship/become-canadian-citizen/citizenship-test.html; June 2022. Who has to take the test and go to the interview, what to study, what happens on test day.

Bibliography

Prime Ministers of Canada; https://thecanadaguide.com/data/prime-ministers; May 2022. List of Prime Ministers of Canada.

Study Guide – Discover Canada – The Rights and Responsibilities of Citizenship; https://www.canada.ca/en/immigration-refugees-citizenship/corporate/publications-manuals/discover-canada.html; June 2022. Discover Canada: The Rights and Responsibilities of Citizenship is used by newcomers to study for the citizenship test. It also contains information about the history of Canada, how our government works, symbols of Canada and its regions.

Index

Aboriginal 5, 13, 15–16, 21, 23, 31–32, 37–38, 41, 49, 52, 56, 65–66, 69, 77, 86, 94, 100, 109

    Aboriginal Affairs 66

    Aboriginal and Treaty Rights 5, 13, 31

    Aboriginal Peoples 5, 13, 109

    Aboriginal Peoples' Rights 5, 109

Acadians 13, 30, 54

Adrienne Clarkson 13, 38, 88, 104

African 7, 22–23, 34

Agnes Macphail 14

Agriculture 43, 45, 49, 51, 57–58, 66, 69

Alberta 34, 36, 48–49, 51, 60, 82

Aldermen 67

Alexander Graham Bell 96

Alexander Roberts Dunn 91

Algonquin 26

Allied Air Effort 8

America 13–15, 21, 23, 30–31, 41, 43, 52, 69, 78, 81, 93, 100. See Also United States, United States of America

American Revolution 21

Anglophones 6, 82, 100

Anne of Green Gables 43

Appalachian Range 45

Arthur Currie 7, 26

Atlantic Provinces 43, 111

Atlantic Trade 45, 58

Atom Egoyan 94

Badlands 49

Banff National Park 49

Baron Tweedsmuir 16

Battle of Amiens 26, 35

Battle of Beaver Dams 19

Battle of Britain 8

Bay of Fundy 45

Beaver 13, 19, 56, 82–83. See Also Symbols of Canada

Bertram Brockhouse 96

Bishop Laval 14–15

Bluebirds 8

Books of Remembrance 65, 86

Branches of Government 65, 110

Brigadier James Wolfe 14

British 6–8, 10, 14, 16, 19, 21–23, 25–28, 31–33, 35, 40–41, 43, 50–51, 56, 62, 69, 76, 78, 81, 86, 91, 95–96, 100, 102, 109, 114

    British Columbia 27, 33, 40, 50–51

    British Commonwealth Air Training Plan 8

    British Commonwealth of Nations 7, 10

    British Empire 6–7, 19, 26, 35, 43, 91

    British North America 32, 41, 62, 69, 76, 78, 81, 100

    British North America Act 69, 78, 81, 100

    British North American Colony 32, 62, 76

    British Parliament 32, 81, 100

    British Rule 23

Bytown 15

Cabinet Ministers 66–67, 73, 110

Canada 3–5, 6–38, 40–54, 56–58, 60–61, 62–66, 68, 70–74, 76–77, 78–81, 82–90, 92–93, 94–96, 98, 100–101, 102, 104, 106, 108–111, 112, 114, 138

    Canada Arts and Culture 94, 96, 98

    Canada Day 63, 86, 93

    Canada Economy 56, 58, 60

    Canada Facts 100

    Canada Geography 40, 42, 44, 46, 48, 50, 52, 54

    Canada Government 62, 64, 66, 68, 70, 72, 74, 76

    Canada Health Act 66

    Canada History 6, 8, 10, 12, 14, 16, 18, 20, 22, 24, 26, 28, 30, 32, 34, 36, 38

    Canada Laws 78, 80

    Canada Symbols 82, 84, 86, 88, 90, 92

Canada-Soviet Summit Series 25, 37, 95

Canadarm 96, 98

Canadian 2, 4–5, 6–9, 13–15, 17, 21, 23–29, 31, 34–38, 41–42, 45–47, 49, 54, 56–58, 60, 63, 65, 70, 73–75, 77, 78–79, 81, 82–84, 88–89, 91–93, 94–96, 98, 100–101, 104, 108–111, 114

    Canadian Astronauts 96

Canadian Charter of Rights and Freedoms 4–5, 38, 81, 109
Canadian Citizens 70, 74, 104, 112, 114
Canadian Citizenship 2, 74, 112, 114
Canadian Citizenship Responsibilities 2
Canadian Constitution 5, 13, 31
Canadian Corps 7, 26, 34–35, 91
Canadian Crown 7, 65, 82, 111. See Also Crown
Canadian Flag 37, 83. See Also Flag
Canadian Forces 7, 14, 65, 82, 111
Canadian Forces Reserves 14
Canadian Heritage and Identity 5
Canadian Justice System 78
Canadian Law 2, 75, 78
Canadian Pacific Railway 15, 34, 83, 93, 101, 110
Canadian Rangers 14
Canadian Red Ensign 83–84
Canadian Rights and Responsibilities 2
Canadian Rights and Responsibilities and Canadian Law 2
Canadian Rights and Responsibilities of Citizenship 2
Canadian Space Agency 96

Canadien 27
Cape Breton Island 17
Caribou 82
Catriona Le May Doan 14, 38, 96
Celtic and Gaelic Traditions 45
Centennial of Confederation 37, 86
Central Canada 43, 45, 58
Chantal Petitclerc 96
Charles Best 98, 110
Charles de Salaberry 19
Charles G.D. Roberts 94
Charlottetown 43
Chateauguay 19
Chief Tecumseh 14
Citizenship 2, 4, 42, 64, 66, 71, 74, 108–109, 112, 114
Civil Code of France 2, 78

Coat of Arms and Motto 82

Cold War 11

Commissioner 67

Communist 11, 37, 101

Confederation 7, 16, 26–28, 33, 37, 43, 62–63, 65, 73, 76, 82, 84, 86, 93, 110.
    See Also Fathers of Confederation

Confederation Bridge 43

Conservative Party 73, 106

Constitution 2, 5, 13, 28, 31, 38, 65, 69, 73, 77, 78, 81

Constitution Act 69, 78

Constitutional Monarchy 7, 65, 73, 82–83, 100, 108, 110

Councillors 67, 69

Count Frontenac 14–15, 30

Courts 7, 65, 79, 82, 111

    Appeal Court 79

    Court of Queen's Bench. See Trial Court

    Supreme Court 79. See Also Trial Court

    Family Courts 79

    Federal Court 79

    Small Claims Courts 79

    Supreme Court 79

Cree 12–13

Criminal Justice 66

Crown 7, 21, 62, 65, 73, 82, 109–111

D-Day 8, 24, 36

Defending Canada 3

Democracy 28, 62, 65, 69–70, 87, 100, 109

Democratic Principles 5, 78, 101

Dene 13, 52

Distinction Between the Sovereign and Prime Minister 73. See Also Prime Minister, Sovereign

District of Keewatin 52

Dominion Day 63, 93

Dominion from Sea to Sea 28, 63, 65

Dominion of Canada 7, 16, 19, 28, 33, 35, 40, 54, 60, 63, 76, 93, 110

Donald Smith 15, 34, 93, 110

Donovan Bailey 38, 96

Due Process 78–79

Duke of Wellington 15, 32

Economy 13, 34, 36, 43, 47, 49, 53, 56–58, 60–61, 139. See Also Economy of Canada
    Economy of Canada 60

Edmonton 37, 49, 56, 95

Education 7, 57, 63, 67, 69

Elected Assembly 67, 81

Elected Legislature 69

Elected Officials 66–67, 69

Elected Representatives 21, 62, 66, 79, 109. See Also Elected Officials

Elections 3, 28, 70, 74–77, 111

Elections Canada 74

Emergency Services 67

Émile Nelligan 94

Emily Carr 15, 94

Emily Stowe 15, 28

England 2, 17, 30, 83

English 2, 5, 6–7, 15, 21, 23, 25, 30, 41–42, 51–52, 65, 77, 78, 81, 82, 84, 86, 100, 109

English Common Law 2, 78

Environment 3, 13, 41, 43, 66, 69, 101, 108

Equality of Women and Men 5, 109

Ernest MacMillan 94

Étienne-Paschal Taché 27

European 6, 13, 16, 23, 25–26, 30, 101, 109

Executive 65, 110

Fathers of Confederation 16, 27, 33, 62–63, 76

Federal 3, 6, 9, 16, 28, 32, 60, 63, 65–67, 69–70, 73–77, 78–79, 100, 110–111
    Federal Government 6, 9, 28, 32, 60, 66–67, 69, 73, 76–77, 78–79, 110
    Federal State 65–66, 100
    Federal Elections 28, 74–77, 111. See Also Voting

Federalism 65

Filip Konowal 91

Firefighting 67

First Nations 6, 13–14, 37, 41, 69

First World War 7, 82, 86, 91

Flag 14, 33, 36–38, 83–84, 96, 100

Flags in Canada 83

Fleur-de-Lys 30, 84

Flying Ace Billy Bishop. See William A. Bishop

Foreign Policy 66

Fort Calgary 24

Fort Edmonton 56

Fort Garry 21, 56

Fort Langley 56

Fort MacLeod 24

Fort Victoria 56

Founding Peoples 16, 100, 109

Founding Principles 2, 78

France 2, 7–8, 13, 16, 24–25, 30, 36, 78, 83–84, 101

Francophones 42, 82, 100

Frederick Banting 98, 110

Fredericton 45

Freed Men and Women 23

Freedom of Association 2, 109

Freedom of Conscience and Religion 2, 109

Freedom of Peaceful Assembly 2, 109

Freedom of Speech and of the Press 2, 109

Freedom of Thought, belief, Opinion and Expression 2, 109

Freedom Under the Law 78

French 5, 6–7, 13–16, 19, 21, 23, 25–28, 30–31, 35, 37, 41–42, 45–47, 49, 54, 56, 62, 65, 77, 78, 81, 82, 84, 86, 100, 109, 111, 139

French Canadiens 19, 100

French Empire 14–15

French Language 28, 62, 109

French Language Rights 28, 62, 109

French Second Empire 65, 86

Frobisher Bay 23, 52

Fur-Trade 13, 56

Gabriel Dumont 16

General Agreement on Tariffs and Trade 56

Geography of Canada 54

Geological Survey of Canada 28, 32

George-Étienne Cartier 27

Gerhard Herzberg 96

Gold Rush 34, 53

Government House 23, 32

Government of Canada 4, 9, 38, 76, 82, 101, 114

Governments in Canada 66. See Also Provincial, Local, Federal, Federal Government, Municipal, Municipal Government

Governor General 13, 16, 21, 25–26, 28, 34–35, 65, 67, 71, 73–75, 88, 95, 102, 104, 110–111, 114

Great Britain 2, 7, 26, 30, 78

Great Canadian Discoveries and Inventions 96

Great Charter of Freedoms 2, 30, 109

Great Lakes 45, 47

Group of Seven 35, 94

Guy Carleton 27, 31

Habeas Corpus 78

Habitants 6

Halifax 17, 23, 31, 45, 58, 76

Harold Innis 96

Head of State 73, 102, 110, 114

Head of the Commonwealth 73

Healey Willan 94

Health Care 57, 66, 69

Helping Others in the Community 3

Henry Woodward 96

Her Majesty 26, 73, 83, 110. See Also Queen, Queen Elizabeth II

Her Majesty's Loyal Opposition. See Official Opposition

Highways 67, 69

History of Canada 30, 32, 34, 36, 38, 114

Honours 23, 37, 86

    Honours System 37, 86

House of Commons 25, 65–67, 70–71, 73–75, 81, 110–111

How a Bill Becomes Law 80

Huron 13, 26, 47

Huron-Wendat 13

Immigration 23, 28, 35, 42, 64, 66, 69, 114

    Black Immigration 23

Important Dates 86

Important People 13. See Also King George V, Bluebirds, John Cabot, First Nations, Arthur Currie, Kainai First Nation, Atom Egoyan, Queen, Queen Elizabeth I, Alexander Graham Bell, Alexander

Roberts Dunn, Wayne Gretzky, Vincent Massey, Terry Fox, Thomas Edison, Kenojuak Ashevak, Emily Stowe, Bertram Brockhouse, Cree, Henry Woodward, Pierre de Monts, William Logan, Sam Steele, Sandford Fleming, Laura Secord, Robert Baldwin, Étienne-Paschal Taché, Sidney Altman, Robert Borden, Charles Best, John Buchan, Joy Kogawa, Joseph Brant, Wilfrid Laurier, Sioux, Margaret Laurence, Charles G.D. Roberts, Marquis de Montcalm, Matthew Evans, Jean-Paul Riopelle, Her Majesty, Queen, Queen Elizabeth II, Lord Durham, Louis Riel, Louis Hémon, Reginald Fessenden, Healey Willan, Founding Peoples, Mohawk Indians, Catriona Le May Doan, Guy Carleton, Roland Michener, Princess Louise Caroline Alberta, Louis-Hippolyte La Fontaine, Members of the National Assembly, Members of the Legislative Assembly, Jacques Cartier, Chantal Petitclerc, Jean Talon, James FitzGibbon, John Graves Simcoe, Marjorie Turner-Bailey, Marshall McLuhan, Chief Tecumseh, Gerhard Herzberg, Gabriel Dumont, Charles de Salaberry, Members of the Provincial (Ontario, Quebec) Parliament, Harold Innis, Mary Ann Shadd Cary, James Naismith, Mark Tewksbury, Members of the House of Assembly, Joseph Howe, Rick Hansen, Lord Elgin, Richard E. Taylor, Martin Frobisher, Mike Lazaridis, Les Automatistes, Jim Balsillie, Lord Grey, Phil Edwards, John McCrae, John Polanyi, Filip Konowal, Huron-Wendat, Group of Seven, Members of Parliament, Joseph-Armand Bombardier, Michael Ondaatje, Montagnais, Rohinton Mistry, George-Étienne Cartier, Robertson Davies, Michael Smith, Ernest MacMillan, Pierre Le Moyne, Stephen Leacock, Samuel de Champlain, Ministers of the Crown, Robert W. Service, Norman Jewison, Robert Hampton Gray, Senators, John Alexander Macdonald, Robert Ross, Isaac Brock, Leonard Tilley, Inuit, Dene, Métis, Oscar Peterson, Frederick Banting, Orville Fisher, Mordecai Richler, Paul Henderson, Pauline Johnson, Napoleon, Paul Triquet, Émile Nelligan, Emily Carr, Legislative, Legislative Assembly, Lieutenant Governor, Mayor, Premier, Queen, Queen Victoria, Prime Minister, Women's Suffrage Movement, Lucy Maud Montgomery, Lord Stanley, Adrienne Clarkson, Agnes Macphail, Bishop Laval, Brigadier James Wolfe, King Francis I, Baron Tweedsmuir, Sovereign, William A. Bishop, William Hall, Donovan Bailey, Wilder Penfield, Donald Smith, John A. Hopps, Duke of Wellington, Volunteers, Newcomers, King George III, Josef Stalin, Royal Canadian Mounted Police

Indian 21, 91

International Trade 66

Inuit 13, 16, 41, 52, 69, 94, 109

Inuktitut Language 16, 109

Iqaluit 23, 52

Iroquoian 16

Iroquois 13, 26, 30

Isaac Brock 23

Jacques Cartier 16, 30

James FitzGibbon 19

James Naismith 34, 95

Jean Talon 14–15

Jean-Paul Riopelle 17, 94

Jim Balsillie 96

John A. Hopps 96

John Alexander Macdonald 27

John Buchan 16, 35

John Cabot 6–7, 17, 30

John Graves Simcoe 18–19

John McCrae 88

John Polanyi 96

Josef Stalin 11

Joseph Brant 17

Joseph Howe 26, 62

Joseph-Armand Bombardier 96

Joy Kogawa 94

Judicial 65, 78, 110

Justice System 3, 78

Kainai First Nation 16

Kenojuak Ashevak 94

King Francis I 16, 30

King George III 5

King George V 19, 35, 60, 93, 102

Knowledge of Canada and Citizenship Criteria 108

Labrador 6, 36, 43, 58, 111

Lady Justice 89

Lake Erie 47

Lake Huron 47

Lake Louise 49

Lake Michigan 47

Lake Ontario 47

Lake Superior 47

Laura Secord 18–19

Laws of Canada 81, 108

Legislative 31, 52, 65, 67, 69, 76, 80, 110

    Legislative Assembly 52, 67, 69

    Legislative Process 80

Leonard Tilley 28, 33, 63, 76

Les Automatistes 17, 36, 94

Liberal Party 73

Lieutenant Governor 19, 67, 73, 110

Local 3, 67, 75, 100, 109, 111. See Also Governments in Canada

London 62, 139

Lord Dorchester 27. See Also Guy Carleton

Lord Durham 21, 62, 109

Lord Elgin 33, 62, 76, 109

Lord Grey 21, 34, 95

Lord Stanley 21, 88

Louis Hémon 94

Louis Riel 21

Louis-Hippolyte La Fontaine 26, 28–29, 33, 62, 76, 109

Lower Canada 21, 32, 54, 62, 76, 81. See Also Quebec

Loyalist 17, 19–21, 27, 31, 45

Loyalists 21, 23, 31, 45, 47

Lucy Maud Montgomery 43

Mackenzie River 52

Magna Carta 2, 30

Major Political Parties 73. See Also New Democratic Party, Liberal Party, Conservative Party

Majority Government 65

Making Laws 80

Manitoba 21, 27, 33–34, 42, 48–49, 54

Manufacturing Industries 47, 57

Maple Leaf 33, 83–84, 101, 111

Margaret Laurence 94

Marjorie Turner-Bailey 23

Mark Tewksbury 96

Marquis de Montcalm 14

Marshall McLuhan 96

Martin Frobisher 23, 30, 52. See Also Frobisher Bay

Mary Ann Shadd Cary 23, 33

Matter of Confidence 66

Matthew Evans 96

Mayor 67

Members of Parliament 66, 70–71, 74, 109

Members of the House of Assembly 69

Members of the Legislative Assembly 69

Members of the National Assembly 69

Members of the Provincial (Ontario, Quebec) Parliament 69

Métis 16, 21, 23, 27, 41, 52, 69, 109

Métis Resistance 16
Michael Ondaatje 94
Michael Smith 96
Mike Lazaridis 96
Military Service 3
Ministers of the Crown 21, 62, 73, 109–110
Minority Government 66
Mobility Rights 5, 109
Mohawk Indians 17
Montagnais 26
Montreal 16, 19, 25, 28, 32, 46, 60, 82, 96
Mordecai Richler 94
Motto 82. See Also Coat of Arms and Motto
Mount Logan 28, 53
Multiculturalism 5, 109
Municipal 67, 70, 75, 79, 111
Municipal Government 67
Municipal Police Departments 79
Napoleon 15, 32
National Anthem 33, 37, 84
National Capital Region 43
National Colours 19, 35, 83, 93
National Defence 8–9, 66
National Motto 82
National Register of Electors 74
National Research Council 98
Natural Resources 43, 47, 56–57, 61, 67, 69
Natural Resources Industries 57
New Brunswick 7, 28, 31, 40, 42, 45, 62–63, 76, 110–111
New Democratic Party 73
New France 7, 25, 84
Newcomers 3, 5, 6, 41, 101, 112, 114
Newfoundland 6, 8, 17, 36, 43, 58, 111
Niagara Falls 23
Norman Jewison 94
Normandy 24, 36. See Also D-Day

North America 13–15, 21, 30, 41, 43, 52, 69, 78, 81, 93, 100

North American Aerospace Defense Command 11

North Atlantic Treaty Organization 10–11

North West Mounted Police 24, 27. See Also Police

Northern Territories 43, 51–52, 67

Northwest Territories 27, 33, 51–52

Nova Scotia 7, 21, 23, 25–27, 30–32, 40, 45, 58, 62–63, 76, 91, 110–111

Nunavut 23, 38, 51–52, 67

O Canada 33, 37, 84–85

Obeying the Law 2, 78, 109

Official Language Rights and Minority Language Educational Rights 5, 109

Official Languages Act 77, 81, 82

Official Opposition 66

Okanagan Valley 51, 57

Old Province of Canada 7, 40, 62, 110

Ontario 7, 20–21, 27, 40, 42, 45, 47, 58, 62, 69, 79, 91, 94, 110. See Also Upper Canada

Opposition Party 66

Order of Canada 25, 37, 86

Orders of Canada and Other Honours 86

Orville Fisher 24

Oscar Peterson 24–25, 37

Ottawa 9, 15, 33–34, 38, 40, 43, 62, 64, 67, 70

Pacific War 9

Parliament 2, 5, 7, 14, 21, 23, 26–27, 32, 37, 64–66, 69–71, 74, 76–77, 78, 81, 82, 86, 100, 109, 111

Parliament Buildings 23, 32, 65, 76–77, 86

Parliamentary Democracy 65, 70, 100

Passport 5, 112

Paul Henderson 25, 37, 95

Paul Triquet 92

Pauline Johnson 94

Peace Arch 40, 87

Peace, Order and Good Government 100

Phil Edwards 25, 35

Pierre de Monts 25–26

Pierre Le Moyne 25. See Also Sieur d'Iberville

Police 7–9, 23–24, 27, 49, 65, 67, 79, 82, 89, 93, 111

Police Services 7, 65, 82, 111

Policing 66–67, 69

Port of Vancouver 51, 57

Prairie Provinces 23, 43, 49

Premier 52, 67

Prime Minister 27–28, 62, 65–67, 71, 73–75, 104, 109–110, 114

Prince Edward Island 31, 33, 43, 76, 111

Princess Louise Caroline Alberta 49

Property and Civil Rights 67, 69

Protecting and Enjoying Canada's Heritage and Environment 3

Province of Canada 7, 32, 40, 62, 76, 110

Provinces and Territories 43, 69, 79, 83

Provincial 2–3, 16, 23, 51, 57, 63, 67, 69–70, 74–75, 78–79, 86, 100, 111, 112

    Provincial Freeman 23

    Provincial Legislatures 2, 67, 78, 86, 100

    Provincial Police Forces 79

Psalm 72 28, 63

Quebec 7, 15–17, 21, 25–27, 30–31, 36–37, 40, 42, 45–47, 54, 58, 60, 62, 65, 69, 77, 79, 81, 84, 86, 92, 94, 110. See Also Lower Canada

Québec City 16, 26, 30–31, 33, 46, 84

Quebec National Assembly 65, 86

Quebecers 16, 25–26, 30, 37, 42, 46

Québécois 25, 81

Queen 7, 23, 26, 30, 33, 37, 43, 49, 52, 65, 70–71, 73, 77, 82, 86, 89, 102, 110

    Queen Elizabeth I 23, 30, 52

    Queen Elizabeth II 26, 37, 43, 77, 82, 102

    Queen Victoria 26, 33, 43, 49, 65, 86, 102

Queenston Heights 23

Recycling Programs 67

Red Poppy 88. See Also Remembrance Day

Reeve 67

Referendum 37–38, 74, 77

Reformers 26–27, 32, 62

Regina 24, 49

Reginald Fessenden 96

Regions of Canada 43. See Also Prairie Provinces, West Coast, Central Canada, Northern Territories, Atlantic Provinces

Reindeer. See Caribou

Remembrance Day 86, 88, 109

Responsible Government 21, 26, 28, 32–33, 62, 76, 109

Richard E. Taylor 96

Rick Hansen 38, 96

Rideau Canal 15, 40

Rights or Freedoms of Aboriginal Peoples 5. See Also Aboriginal, Aboriginal Peoples' Rights

Roaring Twenties 57, 60

Robert Baldwin 26, 62

Robert Borden 28, 76, 106

Robert Hampton Gray 92

Robert Ross 23, 32

Robert W. Service 53

Robertson Davies 94

Rocky Mountains 49

Rohinton Mistry 94

Roland Michener 25–26, 104

Royal Anthem of Canada 89

Royal Canadian Air Force 8, 91

Royal Canadian Army Medical Corps 8

Royal Canadian Mounted Police 8–9, 23, 49, 79, 89, 93, 111

Royal Canadian Navy 8

Royal Flag 83. See Also Flags in Canada

Royal Military College 33, 83

Royal Proclamation 5, 31, 63

Rule of Law 2, 5, 73, 78, 100–101

Sam Steele 22–23

Samuel de Champlain 25–26, 30

Sandford Fleming 98

Saskatchewan 12, 21, 34, 48–49, 58, 82

    Saskatoon 49

Scales of Justice 79, 89

Second World War 8, 25, 92

Secret Ballot 75

Section 15 of the Citizenship Regulations 108

Senate 70–71, 80

Senators 71

Service Industries 57

Serving on a Jury 3, 109

Shared Government Responsibilities 69

Sidney Altman 96

Sieur d'Iberville 25. See Also Pierre Le Moyne

Sioux 13

Sir Arthur Currie. See Arthur Currie

Sir Charles G.D. Roberts. See Charles G.D. Roberts

Sir Ernest MacMillan. See Ernest MacMillan

Sir Étienne-Paschal Taché. See Étienne-Paschal Taché

Sir Frederick Banting. See Frederick Banting

Sir George-Étienne Cartier. See George-Étienne Cartier

Sir Guy Carleton. See Guy Carleton

Sir Isaac Brock. See Isaac Brock

Sir John Alexander Macdonald. See John Alexander Macdonald

Sir Leonard Tilley. See Leonard Tilley

Sir Louis-Hippolyte La Fontaine. See Louis-Hippolyte La Fontaine

Sir Robert Borden. See Robert Borden

Sir Sam Steele. See Sam Steele

Sir Sandford Fleming. See Sandford Fleming

Sir Wilfrid Laurier. See Wilfrid Laurier

Sir William Logan. See William Logan

Skagway 53. See Also Yukon, Yukon Territory, Yukon, Yukon Railway

Slavery 19, 23, 31–32, 101

    Anti-Slavery 23, 101

    Escaped Slaves 23

Social and Community Health 67

Sovereign 26, 65, 67, 70–71, 73, 89, 110

Soviet Union 11

SPAR Aerospace 98

Sports 25, 88, 95

    Canadian Football 21, 34, 88, 95

    Clarkson Cup 13, 38, 88

    Curling 88

    Edmonton Oilers 37, 95

    Grey Cup 21, 34, 95

    Hockey 21, 31, 34, 37–38, 88, 95

    Ice Hockey 31, 88

    National Hockey League 21, 34, 88

    Lacrosse 88

    Popular Sports 88

    Soccer 88

    Stanley Cup 21, 34, 88

St. Jean Baptiste Society 82

St. John River System 45

St. John's 43

St. Lawrence River 16, 45–46

Stephen Leacock 94

Study Questions and Answers 108, 110, 138

Symbols 82–84, 86, 88–90, 92–93, 108, 111, 114. See Also Symbols of Canada

Symbols of Canada 93, 108, 114

Taking Responsibility for Oneself and One's Family 2, 109

Territorial 3, 5, 21, 53, 69–70, 75, 100, 112

Territorial (Territories) 67, 69, 111

Territorial Rights 5

Terry Fox 95

The Hudson's Bay Company 33, 56, 82–83

Thomas Edison 96

Timeline. See Economy of Canada, Symbols of Canada, Government of Canada, History of Canada, Laws of Canada, Geography of Canada

Toronto 14, 17–19, 23, 26, 32, 47, 57, 82, 85, 91, 94, 98, 110, 138. See Also York

Traffic Courts 79. See Also Courts

Transatlantic Slave Trade 100. See Also Slavery

Transportation 57, 67

Treaty 5, 10–11, 13, 31

Trial Court 79. See Also Courts

Underground Railroad 101

Union Jack 83. See Also Flags in Canada

United Canada 25, 33, 62, 76, 81

United Empire Loyalists 45, 47

United Nations (UN) 11

United States 11, 15, 21, 31–32, 40, 47, 56–57, 61, 100. See Also America

United States of America. See America

Unwritten Constitution 2, 78

Upper Canada 19, 21, 27, 31, 62. See Also Ontario

Utilities 67

Victoria 26, 33, 43, 49, 51, 56, 65, 86, 89, 91, 102, 110. See Also British, British Columbia, Victoria Cross, Queen, Queen Victoria

Victoria Cross 89, 91, 110

Vietnam War 101

Vincent Massey 28, 104

Visual Arts 94

Volunteers 3, 14

Voting 3, 34, 54, 70, 74–75, 111, 112

    voters' list 74, 111

    Voting in Elections 3

War of 1918 7

Washington, D.C. 23

Wayne Gretzky 37, 95

West Coast 13, 15, 43, 51, 94

White House 23, 32. See Also Washington, D.C.

White Pass 53

Whitehorse 53. See Also Yukon, Yukon Territory

Wilder Penfield 96

Wilfrid Laurier 28, 86, 106

William A. Bishop 91

William Hall 90–91

William Logan 28, 32, 53

Winnipeg 49, 56, 58

Women's Suffrage Movement 15, 74

World Trade Organization 56

York 7, 19, 23, 32, 97. See Also Toronto

Yukon 34, 51, 53

    Yukon Railway 53

    Yukon Territory 34, 53

ND

Design and composition
André Akinyele, André Akinyele Studios, Toronto, Canada

Set in Times New Roman (courtesy of Monotype) and Avenir (courtesy of Linotype)

The fonts are available in various formats from Monotype (www.monotype.com) and Linotype (www.linotype.com)

Times New Roman
(Serif / Old Style Serif)
Stanley Morison and Victor Lardent

In 1931, The Times of London commissioned a new text type design from Stanley Morison and the Monotype Corporation. The new design was supervised by Stanley Morison and drawn by Victor Lardent. Morison used an older typeface, Plantin, as the basis for his design, but made revisions for legibility and economy of space. As the old type used by the newspaper had been called Times Old Roman, Morison's revision became "Times New Roman." The Times of London debuted the new typeface in October 1932, and in 1933 the design was released for commercial sale. Times New Roman continues to be popular due to its versatility and readability.

Avenir
(Sans Serif)
Adrian Frutiger

Adrian Frutiger designed Avenir in 1988, after years of having an interest in sans serif typefaces. In an interview with Linotype, he said he felt an obligation to design a linear sans in the tradition of Erbar and Futura, but to also make use of the experience and stylistic developments of the twentieth century. The word Avenir means 'future' in French and hints that the typeface owes some of its interpretation to Futura. But unlike Futura, Avenir is not purely geometric; it has vertical strokes that are thicker than the horizontals. These nuances aid in legibility and give Avenir a harmonious and sensible appearance for both texts and headlines.

CPSIA information can be obtained
at www.ICGtesting.com
Printed in the USA
LVHW071818140922
728390LV00031B/479